*

POEMS
and
THE SPRING OF JOY

MARY WEBB has also written

PRECIOUS BANE

SEVEN FOR A SECRET

THE HOUSE IN DORMER FOREST

ARMOUR WHEREIN HE TRUSTED

THE GOLDEN ARROW

GONE TO EARTH

Published by E. P. DUTTON & CO., INC.

MARY WEBB

*

POEMS
and
THE SPRING OF JOY

WITH AN INTRODUCTION BY
WALTER DE LA MARE

New York
E. P. Dutton & Company, Inc.

Contents

INTRODUCTION   Page 13
   BY WALTER DE LA MARE

POEMS

GREEN RAIN	23
MISCHIEF: TO A BEE	24
FOXGLOVES	25
THE WATER OUSEL	26
STARLINGS	27
FAIRY-LED	28
THE SECRET JOY	29
IN APRIL	30
THE HAPPY LIFE	32
'YOU ARE VERY BROWN'	33
MARKET DAY	34
ROSE-BERRIES	36
IN DARK WEATHER	37
THE GARDEN IN WINTER	38
SNOWDROP TIME	39
A RAINY DAY	40
THE SPIRIT OF EARTH	41
TO LIFE	42
'LIKE A POPPY ON A TOWER'	43
PRESENCES	44
A NIGHT SKY (1916)	45
THE PLAIN IN AUTUMN	46
THE ELF	47
MY OWN TOWN	49
THE WOOD	51

7

	Page
VIROCONIUM	53
SWALLOWS	55
HEAVEN'S TOWER	56
DUST	58
THE WATCHER	59
THE LITTLE HILL	61
THE FALLEN POPLAR	62
THE ELFIN VALLEY	63
A SUMMER DAY	64
'THE BIRDS WILL SING'	65
FAREWELL TO BEAUTY	66
THE HILLS OF HEAVEN	67
GOOD-BYE TO MORNING	68
WHY?	69
BEYOND	70
SAFE	71
TO THE WORLD	72
A FAREWELL	73
THE NEIGHBOUR'S CHILDREN	74
AN OLD WOMAN	75
GOING FOR THE MILK	76
TO A LITTLE CHILD BEGGING	77
ANNE'S BOOK	78
ON RECEIVING A BOX OF SPRING FLOWERS IN LONDON	80
FREEDOM	81
SPRING IN THE WEST	82
TO A POET IN APRIL	83
TO A BLACKBIRD SINGING IN LONDON	84
THE LITTLE SORROW	85
TREASURES (FOR G. E. M.)	86

8

THE DIFFERENCE   Page 87
HUNGER   88
WINTER SUNRISE   89
THE LAD OUT THERE   90
TO MOTHER (CHRISTMAS, 1920)   91
ALONE   92
EROS   93
WHEN THE THORN BLOWS   94
'HOW SHORT A WHILE'   95
'BE STILL, YOU LITTLE LEAVES'   96
'AH, DO NOT BE SO SWEET!'   97
AUTUMN   98
NOVEMBER   99
HUMBLE FOLK   100
WINTER   102
THE THOUGHT   103
LITTLE THINGS   104
THE SHELL   105
A HAWTHORN BERRY   106
THE SNOWDROP   107
THE VISION   108
THE VAGRANT   109
THE WILD ROSE   111
THRESHOLDS   112
THE DOOR   113
THE LAND WITHIN   114
THE ANCIENT GODS   116
COLOMEN   118

9

THE SPRING OF JOY

VIS MEDICATRIX NATURÆ   Page 127

JOY –

    THE JOY OF MOTION   139
    THE JOY OF MUSIC   151
    THE JOY OF FRAGRANCE   160

LAUGHTER   171

BEAUTY –

    THE BEAUTY OF FORM   185
    THE BEAUTY OF SHADOW   195
    THE BEAUTY OF COLOUR   202

'YOU WHOM CARE IN PRISON KEEPS, AND SICKNESS DOTH SUPPRESS'   215

POPULUS TREMULA   225

FRUITS OF THE EARTH   231

ROOTS   239

THE CROCKMAN   247

Note

Of the Nature Studies in this volume, 'The Spring of Joy' was published in book form by Messrs. J. M. Dent & Co., in 1917. 'Fruits of the Earth' first appeared in the *Nation*, 'Roots' in the *Spectator*, and 'The Crockman' in *Now and Then*. 'Populus Tremula' is hitherto unpublished.

Introduction

'I HAVE,' said Thoreau,[1] 'a commonplace book for facts and another for poetry, but I find it difficult always to preserve the vague distinction that I had in mind, for the most beautiful and difficult facts are so much the more poetry and *that* is their success . . .'

For Mary Webb there seems to have been either no such vague distinction or no such difficulty. The mere statement of facts that she was interested in is poetical in effect. 'The pollen grain of chicory – an outer and inner hexagon united by rays – is a rose-window in a shrine of lapis lazuli. It needs no light behind it, for it illumines itself.' Few observers have taken the pains to describe an object so minute in terms so precise, yet the words are poetical in effect; they are charged with life and significance, and only a loving rapture in the thing itself could have found them for this purpose.

Sometimes the thing seen is very near home: 'When a cherry blossom falls down the chequered steeps of the tree, a little mournful shadow goes with her.' And sometimes it has come back from a long imaginative journey: '. . . The dwale – that lurid amphora, where the death's-head moth, with its weird form and enchanted purples, drinks under the white light of the

[1] *The Heart of Thoreau's Journals.* Edited by Odell Shepard.

13

moon, and, if it is touched, cries out like a witch in a weak, strident voice.' Or, 'When, long ago, Odoric of Pordenone left the snowy Alps for the Himalayas, snow crystals of the same forms still fell around him.'

Poetical though such fragments are, they are expressed in what, since it is not verse, must be called prose. But Mary Webb being a poet is always a poet when her interest reaches a certain creative intensity, and the poetical in her writing is only a question of degree. It is an intensity that reveals itself not only in the presence of her few rarities, though these were equally her own, but of merely the common things in life which we share with the May-fly, the sparrow, the grass and the stars. It was her birthright.

'As a child,' she said, 'I remember standing awestricken at the strange beauty of a well-known field in the magic of a June dawn.' So had Traherne; so had William Blake. The world is any man's, and apparently inexhaustible, but all that we know of it is what has been 'transmuted into the substance of the mind.' We make of it what we imagine. 'O God! I could be bounded in a nut-shell, and count myself a king of infinite space, were it not that I have bad dreams.' Other Hamlets, other dreams: 'Whoever cares to look may see his neighbour's barn standing in the celestial radiance of *Revelations* or the fantastic brilliance of elfdom.' 'Quite early on a summer morning, if you look down an ugly street in a busy town, you will scarcely know it.'

Not that such in-sight – and who is to say what are its limitations? – is the reward of indolence. 'Evening after evening, in the summer, I have gone to see the white clover falling asleep in the meadow.' Nor is it all pure joy. 'Such beauty brings a longing (almost a torment to some minds) to be absorbed in nature, dissolved in it even to the losing of personality.' So again: 'The sun makes each leaf transparent, and the whole picture is ardent as the face of some angel of a flaming star. As the spirit strives to gather some of the beauty, it longs to be less finite, less bounded.'

With this heart to love and mind to labour, Mary Webb had in her service rarely delicate senses. All poets are for their own purposes good 'observers'; though most of their 'notes,' maybe, take themselves. But by no means all poets are very exact and comprehensive observers. Mary Webb, whose world was 'a place of almost unbearable wonder,' had senses almost microscopic in their delicacy. She could – most rewardful of feats – seize the momentary. 'It may be all illumined, like a sombre pine at the advent of wood-pigeons.' That for sight. And for sound: 'The peewits wheel and call continually, and from amid the ripple of their wings their cry sounds lost and lovely as some Naiad's voice beneath running water.' And this of the wind – with how far a journey: 'It is like a whisper in the night, when you cannot tell whether a child or a man is speaking. . . . We never see the gates of its dark house swing open, nor watch it fall beyond the waters into its tomb beneath the yellow sunset.' And for scent she tells of the resinous sweetness of agrimony on a

15

dusty highway in July; the curious redolence of a rock in hot weather.

In these moods she had no need of 'fine' writing – the writing that is pitched above the voice. Her imagination went abreast with her feeling, and her words embodied both. *The Spring of Joy* wells over with a grave and sweet happiness, the happiness 'of the minds of the simple-hearted, who are the Magi of the world.' Trees, leaves, buds, flowers, fruits; country scenes and ways and work and pleasures; wind and waters, cloud, meadow and woodland; these are its never-failing joy.

It was written, 'a little book of healing,' for a definite audience – an audience whose bodiless presence cannot but be a little intrusive at times, simply because it breaks into the writer's (and reader's) solitude. There is little of the 'indoors' in it, and only such passing references as 'the fœtid haunts of the money-grubbers' to a way of human existence, which she examines more closely in her novels. Its 'problems' are those of peace and truth, of life and death, such as we can rarely face except when we are alone.

Its humour is shared with the long-tailed tit and the dewdrop globed in a buttercup rather than with anything less secret; for 'laughter need not be lost to those that are cut off from their fellows.' But that there were, as with Abel Woodus in *Gone to Earth*, 'dark places' in her soul is clear. 'The men and women who most of all need peace are those who are smitten with some incurable disease.' That we know was not a byword; but as she herself said of Abel: 'It is the dark places of the soul that are the very core of art and its substance.'

The personal experience thus recorded is not only the essence of her fiction, it is also what her poems are 'made of,' and few writers indeed have left behind them so rich a posthumous gift. And though all that she wrote is suffused with poetry, the fine formal difference between her prose and her verse is usually vital, and is not the less essential for being difficult to specify. Phrases alien to the one are the very idiom of the other. Yet both are perfectly 'natural' – she has learned the language. And even though an apparent spontaneity may be only apparent, this poetry is at its best when it *seems* most spontaneous. In any case the meaning conferred, as it were, by rhythm, cadence, sequence of sound and so on is that of the imagination itself; why so seldom acquired, who can say?

> Memoried deep in Hybla, the wild bee
> Sings in the purple-fruited damson tree . . .

> And here's the aconite – a golden moon,
> Shining where all her raying leaflets meet . . .

It is the transmutation that Thoreau speaks of at a further remove:

> There are the twisted hawthorn trees,
> Thick-set with buds, as clear and pale
> As golden water or green hail . . .

Like *The Spring of Joy* the poems are chiefly concerned with the moods and scenes of solitude, and only rarely, but with how passionate a tenderness and generosity, with others – 'Treasures,' 'A Farewell,' 'Ah, do not be so sweet,' 'Why?' 'The Neighbour's Children.' For the most part they are simple, happy, tender, pathetic, and of the lovely earth, but there remain a few – the most original and the finest, as I think – that have for origin the life and experience that is of dreams, whether daydreams or of the night, but which is yet surely as 'real' as anything that can be tested by the usual senses. Such poems, for example, as 'Viroconium,' 'Heaven's Tower,' 'The Vagrant,' 'The Land Within,' 'The Ancient Gods,' and 'Colomen' – one of those romantic 'beginnings' that Mary Coleridge delighted in, and that is not the less the writer's idiom because the ghosts of Christina Rossetti and Coleridge himself haunt its cadences.

But any writing *about* poetry, however well-intended it may be, cannot but resemble beating the air. It can do little but attempt to give reasons for a delight that needs none. And Mary Webb's poems are more than usually her very self's. I cannot remember the first occasion of our knowing one another, and alas, owing to illness, we seldom met during the year or so before her death. But her presence is as clear as ever it was. She brought her own quietness into a room – bright blue eyes, fair brown hair, small hands; bird-like, demure. She loved to listen to others talking quite as much as to talk herself, but her own talk had an extraordinary eagerness and vivacity. Then her nervousness was no more, and she shared her own intense interest and her own happiness.

18

Her gentle yet ardent company, no less than her books, revealed one clear assurance:

> I love all beauteous things,
> I seek and adore them;
> God hath no better praise,
> And man in his hasty days
> Is honoured for them . . .

WALTER DE LA MARE

POEMS

Green Rain

INTO the scented woods we'll go
And see the blackthorn swim in snow.
High above, in the budding leaves,
A brooding dove awakes and grieves;
The glades with mingled music stir,
And wildly laughs the woodpecker.
When blackthorn petals pearl the breeze,
There are the twisted hawthorn trees
Thick-set with buds, as clear and pale
As golden water or green hail –
As if a storm of rain had stood
Enchanted in the thorny wood,
And, hearing fairy voices call,
Hung poised, forgetting how to fall.

Mischief

TO A BEE

O BEE !
While I believed you gathering in the sun
Nectar so busily,
What have you done?

My violet,
More white than well bleached linen, you have kissed:
Her white she must forget
In amethyst.

See, see,
How you have meddled with the snowy clover,
Making her ivory
Blush like a lover!

My primroses,
That gave a greenish, pale moonshine,
O mischief-making bees!
Are red as wine.

Foxgloves

THE foxglove bells, with lolling tongue,
Will not reveal what peals were rung
In Faery, in Faery,
A thousand ages gone.
All the golden clappers hang
As if but now the changes rang;
Only from the mottled throat
Never any echoes float.
Quite forgotten, in the wood,
Pale, crowded steeples rise;
All the time that they have stood
None has heard their melodies.
Deep, deep in wizardry
All the foxglove belfries stand.
Should they startle over the land,
None would know what bells they be.
Never any wind can ring them,
Nor the great black bees that swing them –
Every crimson bell, down-slanted,
Is so utterly enchanted.

The Water Ousel

WHERE on the wrinkled stream the willows lean,
And fling a very ecstasy of green
Down the dim crystal, and the chestnut tree
Admires her large-leaved shadow, swift and free
A water ousel came, with such a flight
As archangels might envy. Soft and bright,
Upon a water-kissing bough she lit
And washed and preened her silver breast, though it
Was dazzling fair before. Then twittering
She sang, and made obeisance to the Spring.
And in the wavering amber at her feet
Her silent shadow, with obedience meet,
Made her quick, imitative curtsies too.
Maybe she dreamed a nest, so safe, so dear,
Where the keen spray leaps whitely to the weir;
And smooth, warm eggs that hold a mystery;
And stirrings of life, and twitterings that she
Is passionately glad of; and a breast
As silver white as hers, which without rest
Or languor, borne by spread wings swift and strong,
Shall fly upon her service all day long.
She hears a presage in the ancient thunder
Of the silken fall, and her small soul in wonder
Makes preparation as she deems most right,
Re-purifying what before was white
Against the day when, like a beautiful dream,
Two little ousels shall fly with her down-stream,
And even the poor, dumb shadow-bird shall flit
With two small shadows following after it.

Starlings

When the blue summer night
Is short and safe and light,
How should the starlings any more remember
The fearful, trembling times of dark December?
They mimic in their glee,
With impudent jocosity,
The terrible ululation of the owls
That prey
On just such folk as they.
'Tu-whoo!' And rusty-feathered fledglings, pressed
Close in the nest
Amid the chimney-stacks, are good all day
If their indulgent father will but play
At owls,
With predatory howls
And hoots and shrieks and whistlings wild and dread.
Says one small bird,
With lids drawn up, cosily tucked in bed,
'Such things were never heard
By me or you.
They are not true.'

Fairy-Led

The fairy people flouted me,
Mocked me, shouted me –
They chased me down the dreamy hill and beat me
    with a wand.
Within the wood they found me, put spells on me and
    bound me
And left me at the edge of day in John the miller's pond

Beneath the eerie starlight
Their hair shone curd-white;
Their bodies were all twisted like a lichened apple-
    tree;
Feather-light and swift they moved,
And never one the other loved,
For all were full of ancient dreams and dark designs on
    me.

With noise of leafy singing
And white wands swinging,
They marched away amid the grass that swayed to let
    them through.
Between the yellow tansies
Their eyes, like purple pansies,
Peered back on me before they passed all trackless in
    the dew.

The Secret Joy

FACE to face with the sunflower,
Cheek to cheek with the rose,
We follow a secret highway
Hardly a traveller knows.
The gold that lies in the folded bloom
Is all our wealth;
We eat of the heart of the forest
With innocent stealth.
We know the ancient roads
In the leaf of a nettle,
And bathe in the blue profound
Of a speedwell petal.

In April, in April
My heart is set
Where the pansy and the violet
And the daffodil,
And close-folded lilies grow
In borders dark with melted snow.
Wakening there from wintry sleep
With every bud I sunward creep.
The empurpled crocuses, that dare
With delicate veins the dawn-cold air,
Cradle me in their chalices
Amid the golden sediment.
There I lie in warm content
And listen to the velvet bees,
Watching their dark blue shadows fall
Along the half-transparent wall.
When the sharp-pointed grasses prick
Upward, all passionate to be free,
I share their conflict, fierce and quick,
With the earthen will; I know their glee.
In the star-tinted pimpernel
I hear the silver tongue of rain;
And learn the perfume thrushes smell,
Which makes their song as keen as pain;
And see, where long-lashed daisies crowd,
New revelations in the cloud.
That is why, when old I grow
And near my end, I shall not know.
For every year my heart is set

With the pansy and the violet
And the daffodil:
Submerged within their beauty, I
Transcend my poor mortality.

The Happy Life

No silks have I, no furs nor feathers,
But one old gown that knows all weathers;
No veils nor parasols nor lace,
But rough hands and a tanned face.
Yet the soft, crinkled leaves are mine
Where pale, mysterious veins shine,
And laced larches upon the blue,
And grey veils where the moon looks through;
The cries of birds across the lawns
In dark and teeming April dawns;
The sound of wings at the door-sill,
Where grows the wet-eyed tormentil;
The ripe berry's witcheries –
Its perfect round that satisfies;
And the gay scent of the wood I burn,
And the slap of butter in a busy churn.

'You Are Very Brown'

ELVES of the hollow and the dewpond still,
Take pity! Gather for me dew as chill
As ice, and glittering-pure as early dawn,
From pink-tipped daisies on the printless lawn,
And the transparent cups of apple-bloom,
And lily bells, to save me from this doom
Of being so brown!
Bring me an unguent made of scented roots;
Pomander of green herbs and scarlet fruits,
Verbena leaves, mallow and melilot,
And balmy rosemary, that I may not
Be brown!
O sweet wild rose,
You have so fair a colour in your face!
Spare me a blush; take from me this disgrace
Of being so brown!
Lilies, you do not guess,
In your pale loveliness,
The grief it is to hear,
In a voice dispassionate and clear,
'You're very brown!'

Market Day

Who'll walk the fields with us to town,
In an old coat and a faded gown?
We take our roots and country sweets
Where high walls shade the steep old streets,
And golden bells and silver chimes
Ring up and down the sleepy times.
The morning mountains smoke like fires;
The sun spreads out his shining wires;
The mower in the half-mown leasur
Sips his tea and takes his pleasure.
Along the lanes slow waggons amble;
The sad-eyed calves awake and gamble;
The foal that lay so sorrowful
Is playing in the grasses cool.
By slanting ways, in slanting sun,
Through startled lapwings now we run
Along the pale green hazel-path,
Through April's lingering aftermath
Of lady's smock and lady's slipper;
We stay to watch a nesting dipper.
The rabbits eye us while we pass,
Out of the sorrel-crimson grass;
The blackbird sings, without a fear,
Where honeysuckle horns blow clear –
Cool ivory stained with true vermilion;
And here, within a silk pavilion,
Small caterpillars lie at ease.
The endless shadows of the trees
Are painted purple and cobalt;

Grandiloquent, the rook-files halt,
Each one aware of you and me,
And full of conscious dignity.
Our shoes are golden as we pass
With pollen from the pansied grass.
Beneath an elder – set anew
With large clean plates to catch the dew –
On fine white cheese and bread we dine:
The clear brook-water tastes like wine.
If all folk lived with labour sweet
Of their own busy hands and feet,
Such marketing, it seems to me,
Would make an end of poverty.

Rose-Berries

THE green pine-needles shiver glassily,
Each cased in ice. Harsh winter, grey and dun,
Shuts out the sun.
But with live, scarlet fire,
Enfolding seed of sweet Junes yet to be,
Rose-berries melt the snow, and burn above
The thorny briar,
Like beauty with its deathless seed of love.

In Dark Weather

AGAINST the gaunt, brown-purple hill
The bright brown oak is wide and bare;
A pale-brown flock is feeding there –
        Contented, still.

No bracken lights the bleak hill-side;
No leaves are on the branches wide;
No lambs across the fields have cried;
        – Not yet.

But whorl by whorl the green fronds climb;
The ewes are patient till their time;
The warm buds swell beneath the rime –
        For life does not forget.

The Garden in Winter

THE winter sun that rises near the south
Looks coldly on my garden of cold clay;
Like some old dotard with a bitter mouth,
Shrugs his grey robe to his ears and creeps away.
Come down the mountains, April! with young eyes,
And roguish daisy-children trooping after,
Draw from the sullen clay red peonies,
Bring back the sun as a stripling full of laughter!

Snowdrop Time

Ah, hush! Tread softly through the rime,
For there will be a blackbird singing, or a thrush.
Like coloured beads the elm-buds flush:
All the trees dream of leaves and flowers and light.
And see! The northern bank is much more white
Than frosty grass, for now is snowdrop time.

A Rainy Day

WITH weights of tears the bluebell broke,
The tall white campion wept in sleeping,
And all the humming honey-folk
A fast were keeping.

The Spirit of Earth

Love me – and I will give into your hands
The rare, enamelled jewels of my lands,
Flowers red and blue,
Tender with air and dew.

From far green armouries of pools and meres
I'll reach for you my lucent sheaves of spears –
The singing falls,
Where the lone ousel calls.

Then, like a passing light upon the sea,
Your wood-bird soul shall clap her wings and flee,
She shall but nest
More closely in my breast.

To Life

FAIR, fierce Life! What will you do with me?
     What will you make me?
     Take me and break me,
     Hurt me, or love me,
But throne me not lonely and safely above thee
     Sweet Life!

Radiant, terrible Life! See now, I offer thee
     Body and spirit.
     Let me inherit
     Agony – wonder:
But leave me not icily, numbly asunder,
     Dear Life!

'Like a Poppy on a Tower'

LIKE a poppy on a tower
The present hour!
The wind stirs, the wind awakes,
Beneath its feet the tower shakes.
All down the crannied wall
Torn scarlet petals fall,
Like scattered fire or shivered glass;
And drifting with their motion pass
Torn petals of blue shadow
From the grey tower to the green meadow.

Presences

THERE is a presence on the lonely hill,
Lovely and chill:
There is an emanation in the wood,
Half understood.
They come upon me like an evening cloud,
Stranger than moon-rise, whiter than a shroud.
I shall not see them plain
Ever again,
Though in my childhood days
I knew their ways.
They are as secret as the black cloud-shadows
Sliding along the ripe midsummer grass;
With a breath-taking majesty they pass,
Down by the water in the mournful meadows;
Out of the pale pink distance at the falling
Of dusk they gaze – remote, summoning, chill;
Sweetly in April I have heard them calling
Where through black ash-buds gleams the purple hi

A Night Sky (1916)

THE moon, beyond her violet bars,
From towering heights of thunder-cloud,
Sheds calm upon our scarlet wars,
To soothe a world so small, so loud.
And little clouds like feathered spray,
Like rounded waves on summer seas,
Or frosted panes on a winter day,
Float in the dark blue silences.
Within their foam, transparent, white,
Like flashing fish the stars go by
Without a sound across the night.
In quietude and secrecy
The white, soft lightnings feel their way
To the boundless dark and back again,
With less stir than a gnat makes
In its little joy, its little pain.

The Plain in Autumn

A SOLEMN land of long-fulfilled desires
Is this, and year by year the self-same fires
Burn in the trees. The untarnished colours keep
The sweetness of the young earth's infant sleep:
Beyond the plain, beneath the evening star,
The burnished hills like stately peacocks are.
Great storms march out. The flocks across the g*
Make their low plaint while the swift shadows pa*
Memoried deep in Hybla, the wild bee
Sings in the purple-fruited damson tree:
And, darkly sweet as Ruth, the dairy maid
By the lean, laughing shepherd is waylaid.

The Elf

A FAIR town is Shrewsbury –
The world over
You'll hardly find a fairer,
In its fields of clover
And rest-harrow, ringed
By hills where curlews call,
And, drunken from the heather,
Black bees fall.
Poplars, by Severn,
Lean hand in hand,
Like golden girls dancing
In elfland.

Early there come travelling
On market day
Old men and young men
From far away,
With red fruits of the orchard
And dark fruits of the hill,
Dew-fresh garden stuff,
And mushrooms chill,
Honey from the brown skep,
Brown eggs, and posies
Of gillyflowers and Lent lilies
And blush roses.

And sometimes, in a branch of blossom,
Or a lily deep,
An elf comes, plucked with the flower
In her sleep;
Lifts a languid wing, slow and weary,
Veined like a shell;
Listens, with eyes dark and eerie,
To the church bell;
Creeps further within her shelter
Of lilac or lily,
Weaving enchantments,
Laughing stilly.

Neither bells in the steeple
Nor books, old and brown,
Can disenchant the people
In the slumbering town.

My Own Town

In this old town I know so well
I have dwelt in heaven and in hell,
And seen its folk go to and fro
With faces of unthinkable woe,
Ferocious as primæval beasts,
Or rapt as angels at their feasts,
When close they press in silver rows
While up and down the chalice goes,
Made of a sapphire, filled to the brim
With God. I have seen them walk like kings
Pondering on majestic things.
And where the gossip gables lean
Chatting, I've met with faces mean
With meanness past all grace or cure.
As long as those blue hills endure,
That stand around the gracious plain
Which circles-in the town, and rain
Marches across the corn, and tears
Weigh down the harvest of our years,
So long what I have seen and felt,
When in its churches I have knelt
And wandered by the evening stream
And seen the April roadways gleam,
Shall live. And when the traffic's hum
Is gone, the busy market dumb
As a winter bee, and all the spires
Are melted in the hungry fires
Of Time, and not a house remains –
Then here, upon the empty plains,

Encircled by the changeless heights,
As changeless through the days and nights
As they, in colours that cannot fade,
Shall stand the town that I have made
With golden house and silver steeple
And a strange uplifted people,
Who in their charmèd streets shall go
Hushed with a tremendous woe
And a joy as deep and vast
As shadows that the mountains cast.
And I shall dwell where once unknown
I passed, and all shall be my own,
Because I built of joy and tears
A city that defies the years.

The Wood

TALL, feathered birches, on the tides of air,
Wash to and fro, like seaweeds fine and fair,
And deep in leaf and blossom from all eyes
The rope-walk of the honeysuckle lies.
There, crimson foxgloves taper slenderly,
And the brown-seeded brake grows ten feet high.
There are strange, flaming toad-stools, and the berries
Of ash and rose, that shine like scarlet cherries.
The rose-day willowherb, in her bridal hour,
Blooms, and the larch sets forth her rosy flower.
Kestrels are there, and tawny foxes play
Amid the shadows in the early day.
Low cry the sheep, and leave their shining fleece
On the long vines of purple blackberries.
High in their minstrel gallery above,
Hidden in fretted leaves, dove answers dove,
And like a distant bell, melodiously
Haunting these glades, the music of the bee
Chimes all the summer. . . . Like a bird, with
        wings
Dusky and silent, I would flit through spring's
Wistful, immaculate colours; through the dream
And hush of summer; down the rush and gleam
Of autumn; and when winter, with a moan,
Swept through the freezing wood aloof, alone,
Prisoning the pine needles in shining, hollow
Cases of ice, yet the brown bird would follow.
Light as a last year's leaf I'd flutter by,
With the sad note of finches in July.

Still should the foxgloves gather, spring by spring;
Still should the feathered birches wash and swing
Upon the tides of air, and in the sun
Each autumn should the little foxes run,
While I in shadow dwelt. Dark on the sky
Should kestrels anchor, watching warily
For small brown birds: but in the meadow green
I'd fearless flit, beneath their gaze unseen.

Viroconium

VIROCON – Virocon –
Still the ancient name rings on
And brings, in the untrampled wheat,
The tumult of a thousand feet.

Where trumpets rang and men marched by,
None passes but the dragon-fly.
Athwart the grassy town, forlorn,
The lone dor-beetle blows his horn.

The poppy standards droop and fall
Above one rent and mournful wall:
In every sunset-flame it burns,
Yet towers unscathed when day returns.

And still the breaking seas of grain
Flow havenless across the plain:
The years wash on, their spindrift leaps
Where the old city, dreaming, sleeps.

Grief lingers here, like mists that lie
Across the dawns of ripe July;
On capital and corridor
The pathos of the conqueror.

The pillars stand, with alien grace,
In churches of a younger race;
The chiselled column, black and rough,
Becomes a roadside cattle-trough:

53

The skulls of men who, right or wrong,
Still wore the splendour of the strong,
Are shepherds' lanterns now, and shield
Their candles in the lambing field.

But when, through evening's open door,
Two lovers tread the broken floor,
And the wild-apple petals fall
Round passion's scarlet festival;

When cuckoos call from the green gloom
Where dark, shelving forests loom;
When foxes bark beside the gate,
And the grey badger seeks his mate –

There haunts within them secretly
One that lives while empires die,
A shrineless god whose songs abide
Forever in the countryside.

Swallows

THE swallows pass in restless companies.
Against the pink-flowered may, one shining breast
Throbs momentary music – then, possessed
With motion, sweeps on some new enterprise.
Unquiet in heart, I hear their eager cries
And see them dart to their nests beneath the eaves;
Within my spirit is a voice that grieves,
Reminding me of empty autumn skies.
Nor can we rest in Nature's dear delight:
June droops to winter, and the sun droops west.
Flight is our life. We build our crumbling nest
Beneath the dark eaves of the infinite,
We sing our song in beauty's fading tree,
And flash forth, migrant, into mystery.

HARK! The wind in heaven's tower
Moaneth for the passing hour.

Heaven's tower is broad and high;
In its quiet chambers lie
Laughing lovers. Rose and apple
Are their cheeks. Pale shadows dapple
All the floors, by night and day,
From sun-ray and moon-ray
Shining through the hearted leaves
Of the dark tree that lips the eaves.
Where the topmost turret ends,
Grey as the parting word of friends,
Sadly sways a silver bell,
And evermore it tolls farewell.
In all weathers, feathered brown
As doves, moaning, up and down,
Hover the disconsolate
Souls that never found a mate.
But within, so safe, so deep
Lapt in joy, the lovers sleep,
Pillowed cool in violets, pansies,
Delicate hopes and tender fancies.
How should they, so closely lying,
With clasping limbs, hear the crying
Of the wind from north or south?
While they murmur, mouth on mouth,
The grievous bell they do not hear,
Every toll a silver tear;

Nor dream they that the mystic, tall
Tree whose leaves like shadows fall
And fill the tower with whispering breath,
Bears the purple fruit of death.

Dust

ON burning ploughlands, faintly blue with wheat
A three-horse roller toils, the wandering dust
A nimbus round it. Shadow-coloured hills
Huddle beyond – hump-shouldered, kingly-headed
Or eel-shaped; sinister, tortured – waiting still,
Beneath the purposeful, secretive sky,
The multitudinous years
That soon or late will melt them.
So I have felt them
In all their static beauty only fit for tears,
Like those that toil along the blood-red weald
With their own death-dust round them for sole glory
Under the falcon wings
Of dawn, the red night's carrion-swoop,
The intolerable emptiness of air.

Long, long ago I thought on all these things:
Long, long ago I loved them.

The Watcher

WHERE the black woods grow sparse and die,
A giant broods against the sky.
The storm his chlamys, and his head
Bent to the spirits of the dead.

The windhover, floating like a leaf,
Passes him safely, clear of grief.
The auburn doves within the wood
Have pondered him and understood.

The wandering breaths of cattle come
Towards his fastness, and the hum
From paper homes of wasps, and cries
Of bees in their refectories.

The evening smoke ascends again
Out of the sapphire-circled plain,
And to the oatfield, pale as wax,
A black swift hurtles like an axe.

There shadow, with her gentle fingers,
Soothes all the dappled land; she lingers
On little croft and ample field,
With their benign and wistful yield.

The Watcher on the summit stands
With a blue goblet in his hands;
He slowly drinks the glimmering years,
The sparkling laughter and the tears.

He is not angered nor forgiving;
He does not sever dead from living,
But sees them all as long gone by,
Returning in futurity.

And still he counts, with stooping head,
The spirits of the living dead—
A soul or two in every field,
And in the furrowed, crimson weald;

And some in every orchard-close,
Who pruned the cherry and the rose,
And waited for the damson sweet,
And plodded through the brittle wheat.

The Little Hill

THIS is the hill, ringed by the misty shire—
The mossy, southern hill,
The little hill where larches climb so high.
Among the stars aslant
They chant;
Along the purple lower slopes they lie
In lazy golden smoke, more faint, more still
Than the pale woodsmoke of the cottage fire,
Here some calm Presence takes me by the hand,
And all my heart is lifted by the chant
Of them that lean aslant
In golden smoke, and sing, and softly bend:
And out from every larch-bole steals a friend.

The Fallen Poplar

NEVER any more shall the golden sun
Make of your leaves, my dainty one,
Ardent shields of silver-green,
With cool blue sky set in between.

Never any more in the chilly night
Your boughs shall move on the sad starlight
Softly unbound by the eager air,
As a lover unbinds his lady's hair.

Never any more, O poplar tree!
Shall dawn awaken your song for me;
For a wind came down from the granite hill
And you, the friend of my heart, lie still.

The Elfin Valley

By this low rock pool, dark and sweet,
Where panting Summer cools her feet,
No creature stirs, except the leaves
That sometimes glide along the air
Like children down a shallow stair,
And nothing strives or grieves.

The long ferns drip from every frond.
Green, round and polished lies the pond,
A mirror for the stooping moon.
Above, the fall is straight and white,
A comet in a sultry night,
Among the leaves of June.

All spell-bound in the drowsy gloom,
Grey-leaved, white-flowered, the mulleins bloom;
And if a swallow suddenly
Should cut the pool with one sharp wing,
Of if a thrush come here to sing,
It seems a prodigy.

A lone green valley, good for sheep,
Where still the ancient fairies keep
Their right of way and copyhold
All night with mullein torches. Far
Within the stream, a dreaming star
Has laid a spell of gold.

A Summer Day

LONG aisles of larches stretch away,
Mysterious, dim;
And in their branches breezes play
A solemn hymn.

Across the glades the larches fling
Their shadows, stirred
Faintly, but no bird lifts a wing,
And sings no bird.

The flecks of sunlight shift and crowd
So goldenly,
And softly faints the last thin cloud
From the blue sky.

'The Birds Will Sing'

THE birds will sing when I am gone
To stranger-folk with stranger-ways.
Without a break they'll whistle on
In close and flowery orchard deeps,
Where once I loved them, nights and days,
And never reck of one that weeps.

The bud that slept within the bark
When I was there, will break her bars –
A small green flame from out the dark –
And round into a world, and spread
Beneath the silver dews and stars,
Nor miss my bent, attentive head.

Farewell to Beauty

'Their being is to be perceived.'

BERKELEY

LET fall your golden showers, laburnum tree!
Break the grey casket of your buds for me —
Soon I shall go where never gold is seen,
And who will be with you as I have been?

Quick with your silver notes, O silver bird!
Wistful, I listen for the song I heard
Many a day, but soon shall hear no more,
For summoning winds are out along the shore.

All things so early fade — swiftly pass over,
As autumn bees desert the withering clover.
Now, with the bee, I sing immortal June;
How soon both song and bee are gone — how soo

Who'll watch the clover secretly unclose?
Finger the sycamore buds, afire with rose?
Trace the mauve veins of the anemone?
Know the peculiar scent of every tree?

Maybe the solemn hill, the enchanted plain
Will be but arable and wild again,
Losing the purple bloom they wore for me —
The dreaming god I could so clearly see.

The Hills of Heaven

WE were in the hills of heaven
But yesterday!
All was so changeless, quiet, fair,
All swam so deep in golden air;
White-tapered chestnuts, seven by seven,
Went down the shady valleys there
Where daffodils are, and linnets play;
And singing streams of yellow and brown
Through golden mimulus ran down.
Ah, haunted were the hills of heaven,
Where no tree falls and none is riven,
Where the frail valley-lilies stay
Becalmed in beauty, every leaf
And every flower!   Ah, bitter grief —
Remembering the hills of heaven
And yesterday!

Good-bye to Morning

I WILL say good-bye to morning, with her eyes
Of gold, her shell-pale robe and crocus-crown.
Once her green veils enmeshed me, following down
The dewy hills of heaven: with young surprise
The daisies eyed me, and the pointed leaves
Came swiftly in green fire to meet the sun:
The elves from every hollow, one by one,
Laughed shrilly. But the wind of evening grieves
In the changing wood. Like people sad and old,
The white-lashed daisies sleep, and on my sight
Looms my new sombre comrade, ancient night.
His eyes dream dark on death; all stark and cold
His fingers, and on his wild forehead gleams
My morning wreath of withered and frozen dreams

Why ?

WHY did you come, with your enkindled eyes
And mountain-look, across my lower way,
And take the vague dishonour from my day
By luring me from paltry things, to rise
And stand beside you, waiting wistfully
The looming of a larger destiny?

Why did you with strong fingers fling aside
The gates of possibility, and say
With vital voice the words.I dream to-day?
Before, I was not much unsatisfied:
But since a god has touched me and departed,
I run through every temple, broken-hearted.

Beyond

Far beyond, far beyond,
Deeper than the glassy pond,
My shivering spirit sits and weeps
And never sleeps.

Like the autumn dove that grieves,
Darkly hid in dove-like leaves,
So I moan within a woe
None may know.

Safe

UNDER a blossoming tree
Let me lie down,
With one blackbird to sing to me
In the evenings brown.
Safe from the world's long importunity —
The endless talk, the critical, sly stare,
The trifling social days — and unaware
Of all the bitter thoughts they have of me,
Low in the grass, deep in the daisies,
I shall sleep sound, safe from their blames and praises.

To the World

You took the rare blue from my cloudy sky;
You shot the one bird in my silent wood;
You crushed my rose – one rose alone had I.
You have not known. You have not understood

I would have shown you pictures I have seen
Of unimagined mountains, plains and seas;
I would have made you songs of leafy green,
If you had left me some small ecstasies.

Now let the one dear field be only field,
That was a garden for the mighty gods.
Take you its corn. I keep its better yield –
The glory that I found within its clods.

A Farewell

BELOVED, once more I take the winter way
   Through solitude's dark mountains, purple and cold
As frozen pansies, toward my house of clay
   Where winds shall drink my tears, and shadows fold.

I dare not dwell so near to ecstasy
   Lest I grow reckless, seeing the dear, the good,
And so, beseeching for it childishly,
   Should spoil its beauty and my womanhood.

Yet will the breathless moments when you smiled,
   Looking upon me, haunt me. It is not well
Remembering, when winter floods are wild,
   Becalmèd lilies and the summer's spell.

Farewell, beloved! Since you have grown too dear,
   I must be gone. I take my pilgrimage
In haste – so much I love you, so much fear.
   Wisdom may grow from tears, peace fall with age.

The Neighbour's Children

THEY run to meet me, clinging to my dress,
The neighbour's children. With a wild unrest
And sobbings of a strange, fierce tenderness,
I snatch them to my breast.
But *my* baby, ah! *my* baby
Weepeth – weepeth
In the far loneliness of nonentity,
And holds his little spirit hands to me,
Crying 'Mother!' and nearer creepeth;
Beats on my heart's lit window anxiously,
Shivering and sobbing, 'Mother, let me in!
Give me my rosy dress, my delicate dress
Of apple-blossom flesh, dark eyes like flowers,
And warm mouth kissed by a red anemone.
Give me my toys – the hills, the seas, the sun,
Loud song, wild winds, the morning's cloudy towers.
Give hands to hold and ears to hear and feet to run.
Give me my lesson books – fear, love and sin –
All hell to brave, all heaven to win!'
Then, shadowy, wild and wan,
A little face peers in,
Except in dreams unknown even to me,
And like a summer cloud is gone.
It is the neighbour's children, playing near,
With voices ringing clear.
But far in twilight, like a moon-awakened bird,
Was that another, fainter laugh I heard?

An Old Woman

THEY bring her flowers – red roses heavily sweet,
White pinks and Mary-lilies and a haze
Of fresh green ferns; around her head and feet
They heap more flowers than she in all her days
Possessed. She sighed once – 'Posies aren't for me;
They cost too much.'
Yet now she sleeps in them, and cannot see
Or smell or touch.

Now in a new and ample gown she lies –
White as a daisy-bud, as soft and warm
As those she often saw with longing eyes,
Passing some bright shop window in a storm.
Then, when her flesh could feel, how harsh her wear!
Not warm nor white.
This would have pleased her once. She does not care
At all to-night.

They give her tears – affection's frailest flowers –
And fold her close in praise and tenderness:
She does not heed. Yet in those empty hours
If there had come, to cheer her loneliness,
But one red rose in youth's rose-loving day,
A smile, a tear,
It had been good. But now she goes her way
And does not hear.

Going for the Milk

GOING for the milk –
A toddling child with skin like curds,
On a May morning in a charm of birds:

Going for the milk
With laughing, teasing lads, at seventeen,
With rosy cheeks and breast as soft as silk –
Eh! what a mort of years between!

Going for the milk
Through my Jim's garden, past the bush o' balm
With my first baby sleeping on my arm:

It's fifty year, come Easter, since that day;
The work'us ward is cold, my eyes be dim;
Never no more I'll go the flowery way,
Fetching the milk. I drink the pauper's skim,
And mind me of those summer days, and Jim
Telling me as my breast was soft as silk –
And that first day I missed to fetch the milk.

To a Little Child Begging

Poor little traveller, lost in night!
God made a miracle, I know,
To give you life – tears and delight,
And ecstasy and ancient woe.
Yet barefoot in the snow you stand,
Beseeching bread with shaking hand.

Poor baby, with your wistful face!
When you are grown a man, and tall,
You'll have the kingly, simple grace,
The smile that makes a festival.
Yet from the dark your hungry eyes
Behold the cook-shop's paradise.

AND SO, Anne Everard, in those leafy Junes
Long withered; in those ancient, dark Decembers,
Deep in the drift of time, haunted by tunes
Long silent; you, beside the homely embers,
Or in some garden fragrant and precise
Were diligent and attentive all day long!
Fashioning with bright wool and stitches nice
Your sampler, did you hear the thrushes' song
Wistfully? While, in orderly array,
Six rounded trees grew up; the alphabet,
Stout and uncompromising, done in grey;
The Lord's Prayer, and your age, in violet;
Did you, Anne Everard, dream from hour to
    hour
How the young wind was crying on the hill,
And the young world was breaking into flower?
With small head meekly bent, all mute and still,
Earnest to win the promised great reward,
Did you not see the birds, at shadow-time,
Come hopping all across the dewy sward?
Did you not hear the bells of Faery chime
Liquidly, where the brittle hyacinths grew?
Your dream – attention; diligence, your aim!
And when the last long needleful was through,
When, laboured for so long, the guerdon came –
Thomson, his *Seasons*, neatly bound in green –
How brightly would the golden letters shine!
Ah! many a petalled May the moon has seen
Since Anne – attentive, diligent, *aetat* nine –

Puckering her young brow, read the stately phrases.
Sampler and book are here without a stain –
Only Anne Everard lies beneath the daisies;
Only Anne Everard will not come again.

So the old, dear freemasonry goes on –
    The busy life, the laughter-under-sod,
The leafy hosts with spear and gonfalon
    Guarding the earthy mysteries of God.

I did not think the violets came so soon,
    Yet here are five, and all my room is sweet;
And here's an aconite – a golden moon
    Shining where all her raying leaflets meet;

And here a snowdrop, finely veined – ah, see!
    Fresh from the artist's hand, and folded close
She only waits the sunshine and the bee;
    Then she will open like a golden rose.

Freedom

WHEN on the moss-green hill the wandering wind
Drowses, and lays his brazen trumpet down,
When snow-fed waters gurgle, cold and brown,
And wintered birds creep from the stacks to find
Solace, while each bright eye begins to see
A visionary nest in every tree –
Let us away, out of the murky day
Of sullen towns, into the silver noise
Of woods where every bud has found her way
Sunward, and every leaf has found a voice.

Spring in the West

Soon amid the inviolable places
Will green, rustling steeples chime again
With the sweet, glassy bell-notes of the wren.
Soon the plain shall lie beneath blue spaces –
Bold and broad and ruddy in the sun,
Long and lean to the moon when day is done.

Soon will come the strange, heart-lifting season
When through the dark, still dawns, where nothing wa
Steals the mysterious whisper of growing grass;
And a joy like pain possesses the soul, without reaso
Between the budding of day and the lapse of night,
With the clear, cold scent of wet starlight.

To a Poet in April

THE world has praised your leafy songs,
And you, in singing them, have made
Rich folk forget their gains and wrongs
And poor folk love the hawthorn shade.
While year by year your fame has grown,
You had one silent friend unknown.

And on those gleamy April days
That hurt my soul with too much bliss
When I am wandering woodland ways,
A-bloom with twining ecstasies,
You speak my joy in silver words
I thought none knew so well, but birds.

So deep within a blossomy cave
With musing blackbirds in the trees,
While snowy petals softly pave
The ground, and thread the rainy breeze,
I share your songs, through charmèd hours,
With my sworn friends, the leaves and flowers.

To a Blackbird Singing in London

SING on, dear bird! Bring the old rapturous pain,
In this great town, where I no welcome find.
Show me the murmuring forest in your mind,
And April's fragile cups, brimful of rain.
O sing me far away, that I may hear
The voice of grass, and, weeping, may be blind
To slights and lies and friends that prove unkind.
Sing till my soul dissolves into a tear,
Glimmering within a chaliced daffodil.
So, when the stately sun with burning breath
Absorbs my being, I'll dream that he is Death,
Great Death, the undisdainful. By his will
No more unlovely, haunting all things fair,
I'll seek some kinder life in the golden air.

The Little Sorrow

WITHIN my heart a little sorrow crept,
And wept, and wept.
Below the lilt of happiest melodies
I heard his sighs,
And cried – 'You little alien in my heart,
Depart! Depart!'

Amid the loud, discordant sounds of fate,
I listening wait –
Not hoping that a song can reach my ear:
But just to hear
That little weeping grief I once bade cease
Would now be peace.

Treasures

(FOR G. E. M.)

THESE are my treasures: just a word, a look,
A chiming sentence from his favourite book,
A large, blue, scented blossom that he found
And plucked for me in some enchanted ground,
A joy he planned for us, a verse he made
Upon a birthday, the increasing shade
Of trees he planted by the waterside,
The echo of a laugh, his tender pride
In those he loved, his hand upon my hair,
The dear voice lifted in his evening prayer.

How safe they must be kept! So dear, so few,
And all I have to last my whole life through.
A silver mesh of loving words entwining,
At every crossing thread a tear-drop shining,
Shall close them in. Yet since my tears may break
The slender thread of brittle words, I'll make
A safer, humbler hiding-place apart,
And lock them in the fastness of my heart.

The Difference

I WALK among the daisies, as of old;
But he comes never more by lane or fold.
The same warm speedwell-field is dark with dew;
But he's away beyond a deeper blue.
A year to-day we saw the same flowers grow –
Last May! Last May! A century ago.

Above the speedwell leans the rosy tree
From which he plucked an apple bough for me.
Not all the blossom on the branches left
Can fill the place of that sweet bough bereft;
And none can fill the heart that loved him so
Last May! Last May! Eternities ago.

Hunger

Not for the dear things said do I weep now;
Not for your deeds of quiet love and duty
Does my heart freeze and starve since you endow
Cold death with beauty.

Just for the look of utter comprehension;
The dear gay laugh that only true hearts know;
For these I would from life's severe detention
Arise and go.

Winter Sunrise

ALL colours from the frozen earth have died,
And only shadow stains the cold, white snow:
But in the air the April tints abide;
Intangibly and radiantly they grow.
There bloom immortal crocuses, beside
. live-rose hedge, and irises that grow
Along a far green inlet – circling wide
Anemone fields where none but stars may go.
The ardours of a thousand springs are there;
Through infinite deeps they quicken, bright and tender:
In that sequestered garden of the air
No icy pall is heavy on the splendour.
Since you are not in the wintry world to love me,
How softly painted flushes Death above me!

The Lad Out There

OH, Powers of Love, if still you lean
Above a world so black with hate,
Where yet – as it has ever been –
The loving heart is desolate,
Look down upon the lad I love,
(My brave lad, tramping through the mire) –
I cannot light his welcoming fire,
Light Thou the stars for him above!
Now nights are dark and mornings dim,
Let him in his long watching know
That I too count the minutes slow
And light the lamp of love for him.
The sight of death, the sleep forlorn,
The old homesickness vast and dumb –
Amid these things, so bravely borne,
Let my long thoughts about him come.
I see him in the weary file;
So young he is, so dear to me,
With ever ready sympathy
And wistful eyes and cheerful smile.
However far he travels on,
Thought follows, like the willow-wren
That flies the stormy seas again
To lands where her delight is gone.
Whatever he may be or do
While absent far beyond my call,
Bring him, the long day's march being through,
Safe home to me some evenfall!

To Mother

WITHIN the doorway of your room to-night
  I stood, and saw your little treasures all
Set out beneath the golden candle-light,
While silver chimes haunted the evenfall.
Here was the robin, very round and bright,
  Painted by one of us with fingers small,
And childish presents, bought with grave delight,
  For many an ancient Christmas festival.
And while I looked, dear mother, I thought of those
Great dreams that men have dreamed – music like
      flame,
The lovely works of many a deathless name,
  Poetry blooming like a fragrant rose;
And knew God kept them in His house above,
As you our gifts, from the greatness of His love.

Alone

THE lonely cuckoo calls
With a long hollow sound among the rocks
Of sun-touched sandstone, and the echo falls
Between the straight red pines to me, and knock:
Upon my heart again and yet again.
It thrills me
With some mysterious mingled joy and pain
That slumbers in the echoing refrain
And stills me.

If only you were here,
We'd go together through the buckler-fern
And watch the nuthatch climbing to his dear;
Then – so that you might follow – I would turn,
And, smiling, mount the steep, and leaning so
Above you,
Await your laughing kiss with eyes a-glow.
Ah! foolish dream – you do not even know
I love you.

Eros

BEFORE his coming thunder breaks;
In plunging fires his way he takes;
Beneath his feet the daisies die,
And night looms darkly in his eye.
 So let him come!
 Let every silver, trilling bird be dumb!
 Let the white daisies drooping lie
 Crushed by his pitiless urgency.

He gives no soft or honied kiss,
Nor sings melodious rhapsodies
Of easy joy and bright reward:
His beauty is a flaming sword.
 So let him come!
 Let every silver, trilling bird be dumb!
 Let the white daisies drooping lie
 Crushed by his pitiless urgency.

When the Thorn Blows

DAWN glimmers white beyond the burning hill
  Where sunbeams light a fire in every tree.
The morning bird is singing clear and shrill;
  And oh, my love! when will you come to me

The daisies whitely sleep 'beneath the dew;
  On the wet road the stones are fair to see;
Cloudy, the blackthorn floats upon the blue;
  And oh, my love! when will you come to me

The wind came walking in the shaken wood;
  He shouted from the mountains and the sea
By the pale thorn he paused, in lover's mood
  And oh, my love! when will you come to me

My heart has blossomed meekly as the thorn;
  It has its dews, and daisies two or three.
The heavens quicken, green as April corn –
  And oh, my love! when will you come to me

'How Short a While'

How short a while – eternities gone by –
It is since book and candle, half the night,
Consumed the hours, and in the first grey light
I turned and strove for slumber wearily:
But the sad past complained too mournfully,
And wept before me till the dawn grew white;
And the stark future, stripped of all delight,
Loomed up so near – I could but wake and sigh.

Now they are gone. I lie with ungirt will
And unlit candle, sleeping quietly.
Love flows around me with its calm and blessing;
I can but let it take me, and be still,
And know that you, beloved, though far from me,
All night are with me – comforting, caressing.

'Be Still, You Little Leaves'

Be still, you little leaves! nor tell your sorrow
To any passing bat or hovering owl
Or the low-splashing, restless water-fowl.
You flowering rushes, sigh not till to-morrow;
Come not, sad wind, out of your caverns eerie
My love is sleeping, and my love is weary.

'Ah, Do Not Be So Sweet!'

Ah, do not be so sweet!
For if you only go across the street
The moment is a year.
I hate the careless feet that hurry on
And know not you are near.
An instant fled – and life so swiftly gone,
And you so very dear.

Ah, do not be so kind!
There is so much of beauty in your mind.
When low your dark head lies
In sleep, I see your brow and mouth possessed
With some old agonies,
And thirst for morning – broken, sad, distressed
Until I see your eyes.

Ah, do not be so dear!
The heavy-handed world, if it should hear
And watch us jealously,
Would steal upon our love's secure retreat
And rob our treasury.
Let us be wise, then; do not be too sweet,
Too dear, too kind to me!

Autumn

WHEN autumn winds are on the hill
  And darkly rides the wasting moon,
I creep within your arms, and still
  Am safe in the golden heart of June.

November

WHEN on my merry garden cold fogs rise
And from these golden trees the blossoms fall;
When in the hollow, painted morning skies
No more the sweet birds call;
When music dies, and colour blurs to grey,
And laughter slips into a sob and fails;
When all my troops of dreams, serene and gay,
Are frozen nightingales –
Where shall I turn, since God is far withdrawn,
And heaven a palace fallen in the sea?
How can I live, a stranger to the dawn?
Ah, who will comfort me?
You, dear, with sadness of unflinching sight,
Behold the pitiful world, the pitiless sky,
Strong in the midst of storm and cold and night,
More great, more brave, than I;
And I could live with sorrow all my days,
Having your word of praise.

Humble Folk

ABOVE our lane two rows of larches lean,
And lissom, rosy pines with wild black hair –
One slim, bright-fingered chestnut in between.
In blossom-time and berry-time and snow
Are muffled sounds of feet that come and go
Forever, from the cones and falling spines
And the sad, homeless rhythm of the pines.
These are our friends; we feel the griefs they
        bear;
We know the larches' thin young April song;
The heavy, dark endeavour of the cone
That goes alone
Among the thick, obliterating dust –
Impelled by something faint and strong
Within her, by the lust
Of death, towards the red and living tree.
Our fingers and the chestnut's touch and hold
The blue light and the gold,
And in a little drop them listlessly.
We know so few things more than these –
The larch that moans in rain
And every March puts roses on again;
The wise, mute chestnut listening to the bees;
The pine
That drinks the icy wind like wine.
We ask no better birth than their brown roots;
We dare not dream of immortality
Unshared by their brown fruits.
And when the wild bee's voice

Grows faint for us, we only ask to lie
Like two straight trees cut down together,
Not fearing any weather,
Too soundly sleeping even to rejoice.

Winter

If I should be the first to go away
Out of the golden sunlight of our peace,
When the dear sacrament of common day
And lowly, love-empurpled tasks shall cease;
When the old books beside the evening fire
Neglected lie, and closed the garden gate,
And from our hill the blossom-tinted shire
Gathers for us an air disconsolate –
Then, oh beloved! hold me close, so close,
Nearer than thought of pain or sad regret;
So wrapped in you, I even should forget
The lifelong dread of parting; and the rose
Of June would flower for me, though cold and slow
And weary on our roof-tree fell the snow.
Speak to me then with that most tender voice,
Wherein I hear the forest murmur fall,
The songs of the corn and velvet-throated doves
That each on each with muted music call,
Minding each other of their leafy loves.
So gathered safe within your voice, your eyes,
Your dear protecting smile, I shall not know
When the black frost sets in, the dark wind cries.
For as the squirrel and the mole, so warm
Within their snow-proof chambers, and the bee
Walled in with summer, wake not, though the storm
Besieges hive and forest – so with me
All will be well; for, sealed in dreamless slumbers,
I shall not know my world is desolate.
Ages may pass, like leaves that no man numbers,
While in the nest of love I hibernate.

The Thought

As a pale moth passes
In the April grasses,
So I come and go,
Softlier than snow.
Swifter than a star
Through the heart I flee,
Singing things that are
And things that cannot be.
I whisper to the mole
And the cold fish in the sea,
And to man's wistful soul
God sendeth me.
As a grey moth passes
In October grasses,
So I come and go,
Softlier than snow.

Little Things

AMONG the purple buds, like laden censers,
Careless upon the wind the catkins swing;
They lay a golden spell upon the morning.
From their soft glee how many trees will spring?

The tiny spiders on wych elms in May,
Of rare pale green; the young and downy bee,
Singing her first low song; the white ant's cradle –
They crowd upon us with their mystery.

The fourfold creamy blackthorn buds are folded
Close on green marvels, as upon a treasure
A child's hand; the five pearl doors open softly –
There's a gold house where some elf takes his pleasure.

On the small pear-bud, with its silver calyx,
Some one (I know not who) has set a cross,
Rosy and glowing.   On that Calvary-rood
Love might hang long, and know not pain or loss.

Fire-white from curtains of intensest blue
The centre of the speedwell gleams; so fair,
So mystic-frail the tremulous pollen-worlds,
Divinity itself seems slumbering there.

The Shell

WHAT has the sea swept up?
Viking oar, long mouldered in the peace
Of grey oblivion? Some dim-burning bowl
Of unmixed gold, from far-off island feasts?
Ropes of old pearls? Masses of ambergris?
Something of elfdom from the ghastly isles
Where white-hot rocks pierce through the flying spin-
    drift?
Or a pale sea-queen, close wound in a net of spells?

Nothing of these. Nothing of antique splendours
That have a weariness about their names:
But – fresh and new, in frail transparency,
Pink as a baby's nail, silky and veined
As a flower petal – this casket of the sea,
The shell.

A Hawthorn Berry

How sweet a thought,
How strange a deed,
To house such glory in a seed –
A berry, shining rufously,
Like scarlet coral in the sea!
A berry, rounder than a ring,
So round, it harbours everything;
So red, that all the blood of men
Could never paint it so again.
And, as I hold it in my hand,
A fragrance steals across the land:
Rich, on the wintry heaven, I see
A white, immortal hawthorn-tree.

The Snowdrop

THREE softly curved white petals veined with light,
Three green-lined sepals, guarding frugal gold,
And all so strong to fold or to unfold!
Snow thunders from the bending pines. How slight
This frail, sheathed stem! Yet all unbent it springs,
So swift in stoopings and recoverings.

In the pale sunshine, with frail wings unfurled,
Comes to the bending snowdrop the first bee.
She gives her winter honey prudently;
And faint with travel in a bitter world,
The bee makes music, tentative and low,
And spring awakes and laughs across the snow.

The Vision

In the busy tongues of spring
There's an angel carolling.
Kneeling low in any place,
We may see the Father's face;
Standing quiet anywhere,
Hear our Lady speaking fair;
And in daily marketings
Feel the rush of beating wings.
Watching always, wonderingly,
All the faces passing by,
There we see through pain and wrong
Christ look out, serene and strong.

The Vagrant

HO came so close then? –
ushed the wet lilac into mellow laughter;
t the smooth blackbird at his golden weaving;
aking no stir at all, no footprint leaving;
avelling westward, all things following after?

ho whispered secrets? –
mpted the worm up from her winter hiding
lie her length in the rain of early summer?
ho cut the leaf-buds open? What new-comer
ld the tall heron the place of her abiding?

me one has been here:
t the rough, drunken wind who shouts and wanders,
ampling the woodpath; neither dawn nor gloaming
r the young airs in cowslip-garlands roaming.
ho was it then? The muted spirit ponders.

ose by the water
rapt in a dream, I saw a faint reflection
e a wayfarer, calm and worn of features,
d in the brown of leaves and little creatures,
rn as the moorland, russet of complexion.

rk in the shadow
thomless eyes met mine with thought unspoken,
stful, yet deep within them laughter lingered.
th sunburnt hands a wooden flute he fingered
der the thorn-tree, where the lights are broken.

Then the green river
Dimmed like a misted mirror; blossom only
Whitened it, on the covert water lying.
Westward along the willows ran a sighing.
Herd-like the clouds went home and left me lonely

Over the meadows
Wild music came like spray upon the shingle;
Piping the world to mating; changing, calling
Low to the heart like doves when rain is falling.
Surely he cut his flute in Calvary's dingle?

I rose and followed
Right to the sunset-bars, yet never found him.
Backward along the edge of night returning
Sadly, I watched the slip of moon upburning
Silver, as if she drank the life around him.

In the dark aspens
Hark! a flute note; so still he's at his playing.
Tawny the furrows lie – his homely vesture.
Labourers pass: I see his very gesture –
Vigorous, tranquil, with his music straying.

Now I know surely
Who set the birds a-fire and touched the grasses –
Silent, without a footprint, no shade throwing.
Infinite worlds his shadow: all things growing
Stir with his breathing, follow as he passes.

The Wild Rose

FIVE pointed sepals with a pearly sheen
Uphold the frail cup's curved transparency,
White-veined below, and flushing tenderly
Towards the brim. A shadow lies between
Each loose-curved petal, and the scent – so keen,
So sweet – is very wine of joy to me.
The humming honey-people eagerly
Enjoy this loving-cup among the green.
We share together, the butterfly, the bee
And I, and the little beetles that gleam and shine.
And yet one more, my spirit whisperingly
Has spoken of, whose banquet is divine.
Deep down within the chalice I can see
The gold He left there as His kingly fee.

Thresholds

So here is come the night of nights!
On every pine a star is kindled.
Too slowly cumbrous summer dwindled;
But now the frostly silence hums
And comfort in the boundless darkness comes
      Along the heights..

Through weary times of brooding harm
We waited. Now the hour is ringing.
In haste we leave the wicket swinging
And whisper, splashing through the mire,
Of music and of colours bright like fire
      At Thresholds Farm.

Up yonder on the hill-side stark
The long sheds crouch beneath the larches.
We smile to think the whole world marches
With us to where the shippen gleams
And flower-pale faces cluster, keen as dreams,
      Against the dark.

We hear the cow-chains lift and fall;
We almost feel the ageless splendour
Of Child and Mother, warm and tender;
We run and softly push the door . . .
The mice go shrieking down the lonely floor,
      The empty stall.

The Door

I HEARD humanity, through all the years,
Wailing, and beating on a dark, vast door
With urgent hands and eyes blinded by tears.
Will none come forth to them for evermore?
Like children at their father's door, who wait,
Crying 'Let us in!' on some bright birthday morn,
Quite sure of joy, they grow disconsolate,
Left in the cold unanswered and forlorn.
Forgetting even their toys in their alarms,
They only long to climb on father's bed
And cry their terrors out in father's arms.
And maybe, all the while, their father's dead.

The Land Within

THIS is a land of forests, and of meres
Stirless and deep, replenished with my tears.
Here the pine harps, and many voices moan
Within the cedar, crying, 'Lone! Alone!'
Sharp on green heaven the green ice peaks arise
Through the deep snows of thawless purities.
Ten thousand stars are drowned within the lake,
Beneath grey ice. And while the branches break,
The million crystals shining there arow
Can never fall, though every tempest blow.
Only the rush, with brown and broken spear,
Tells of the host of summer mustering here,
Where now the reeds, encrusted stiff with glass,
Sound a faint music, faintly sigh 'Alas!'
Where are the birds that with blue flash would make
Traffic between blue sky and bluer lake,
Ripping the water with a long, keen wing,
Then setting rosy breasts arow to sing?
O, they are fled, my soul! Fled far away
To some gold tree in Spain or Africa.

Was there a sound of leaves here once, and streams
Gurgling on pebbles? (In dreams, my soul! in dreams)
Galleons of golden lilies then could ride
Safely, though coot and moorhen stirred the tide,
Swimming with all their young; and loud sweet cries
Fell from the mountains where the curlew haunted
Green mossy cwms, sun-drenched and thrice en-
    chanted;

And somewhere in the lake's confused reflections,
Remote and fair as childhood's recollections,
Smothered in wavering lilac leaves, and blurred
With bloom, the shadow of a gable stirred
With every tide, and a twisted chimney flowered
In pale blue smoke, that in the water towered
Downward. And through those deeps, pillared and
　　aisled,
Came a brown woodman, and a boy who smiled,
Running towards the shifting wicket-gate,
And waved an under-water hand, to spy
One leaning from the casement – that was I.

Where was that cottage with its lilac trees,
Its windows wide, its garden drowsed with bees?
Where stood the echoing glade whence the faggot came
To turn the evening hours to one warm flame?
And that brown woodman, where and whence was he –
That woodman, with the eyes that dazzled me
Far more than rosy fire or golden gleams
Of April? O, in dreams, my soul! in dreams.

The Ancient Gods

CERTAINLY there were splashings in the water,
Certainly there were shadows on the hill,
Dark with the leaves of purple-spotted orchis;
But now all's still.

It may be that the catkin-covered sallow,
With her illusive, glimmering surprise,
Pale golden-tinted as a tall young goddess,
Deceived my eyes;

And the white birches wading in the margin,
Each one a naked and a radiant god,
Dazzled me; and the foam was flung by currents
Where no feet trod.

Only I know I saw them – stately, comely,
Within the leafy shadows of the stream;
They woke amid the shallow, singing water
A fading gleam.

They left no trail for any beast to follow,
No track upon the moss for man to trace;
In a long, silent file up-stream they vanished
With measured pace.

The hollow water curved about their ankles
Like amber; splashes glistened on their thighs;
Sun barred their lifted heads and their far-seeing
Yet sightless eyes.

Some were like women, with deep hair of willows,
Bare breasts and gracious arms and long, smooth hips,
And the red roses of desire half frozen
Upon their lips:

But most were massive-browed and massive-shoul-
    dered
And taller than the common height of men.
They went as those that have not home nor kindred,
Nor come again.

Still, where the birches fingered their reflection,
The thrushes chanted to the evening sky;
Still the grey wag-tails raced across the shingle
As they went by.

Beyond the furthest of the saffron shallows
I lost them in the larches' rainy green,
And only saw the stretches of marsh-mallows
Where they had been.

You say the sallow and the birch deceived me:
But I know well that I beheld to-day
The ancient gods, unheralded, majestic,
Upon their way.

Colomen

THE doves that coo in Colomen
Are never heard by mortal men
But when a human creature passes
Underneath the churchyard grasses.
In deep voices, velvet-warm,
They tell of ancient perils, storm
Long hushed, and hopes withered and dead,
And joys a long while harvested.

There was a lady small and thin
(Oh, grave! Why did you let her in?)
Her voice was sad as a dove's, her feet
Went softly through the yellow wheat,
Like stars that haunt the evening west.
Hers was the tall, round, sunny cote
Whence, as she called, her doves would float
Softly, on arm and shoulder rest,
Until the lady, leaning so,
Under the feathers of rose and snow,
Wing of azure and purple plume,
Was like a slim tree bent with bloom.

And still, at Colomen, they say,
When midsummer has stolen away
The last arch primrose, and swiftly fall
Hawthorn petals, wan as a pall,
And the grave blackbirds, that of late
Shouted the sun up, meditate,

You hear about the ruined cote
A mighty, muted sound of wings,
And faint, ghostly flutterings.
Then, if your death is near, you see
A lady standing like a tree
Bent down with blossom. Long ago
Her little joy, her long woe!

In an April dawn of rose and flame
A poor, travelling painter came
Through tasselled woods, and in the tower
Beheld the lady, like a flower –
A pale flower beneath the hill,
Trembling when the air is still,
Broken when the storms are wild.
The lady looked on him, and smiled.
Woe, woe to Colomen,
Where never lovers come again,
Laughing in the morning air!

Dew decked the lady's hair
Because the lilac, purple and tall,
Saw her beauty and let fall
All her silver, all her sweet.
In dove-grey dawns their lips would meet
In the room beneath the tower
Where the drowsy sunlight smote
Seldom, and the air would creep
Stealthily and half asleep,

119

While stillness held the dancing mote,
And croonings fell from the ivied cote
With a musical, low roar,
Like summer seas on a fairy shore.

The boding wind had moaned of loss;
The boding shadow laid a cross
From the barred window to their feet;
The doves made a heart-broken, sweet
Clamour of some eerie thing.
They did not hear nor understand
How soon love is withered away
Like a flower on a frosty day!

Early in a summer dawn
When the shadows of the doves were drawn
Down the roof, and from the clover
The bees' low roar came up, her lover
Finished her portrait, thin and small
And pale, with an ethereal
Sweet air, because he had seen her soul
Come to the threshold when she stole
To meet him. There forever she stood
Like a silver fairy in a wood
Or a maytree in the moonlight.
He told her of his dream's delight,
How they would dwell alone, aloof,
With doves crooning on the roof.

He had painted through a sapphire June
Into a thunderous dark July.
Alas! How fleet is spring! How soon
From all their little windows fly
The doves of joy! In an evil hour
Her sister saw him leave the tower.

For all her simple country grace,
Hers was a haughty, lordly race.
When night was thick and black above,
They sent the press-gang for her love.

All day, beside the memoried cote
She lay so still they thought her dead,
Her doves, that wheeled above her head.
But in her eyes a wild, remote,
Inhuman sorrow slumberèd.

When next the clover called the bee,
Where was she? Ah, where was she?

She dragged her leaden limbs across
The grey lawns, to hear the sound
That turned a sword within her wound
And made her agony of loss
So keen that if she held her breath
She almost heard the feet of death.

When all her thronging pigeons cooed
Around, with outspread arms she stood.
She seemed a pale and slender tree,
Bent with snow and not with bloom –
Bent lower towards the tomb.

She would be free of the distress
That men call joy, the littleness
That men call life – as birds are free.
So in the dewy morning hour
She hangèd herself within the tower,
Beside her portrait, spirit-fair,
With these words written: 'We come again,
And ours the house of Colomen.'

Her cousins came and found her there,
While high against the painted dawn
Her pigeons – rosy, white and fawn,
Coal-black and mottled – wheeled in the air.
But while they gazed, weeping aloud,
Around the tower a silence fell.
The doves wheeled high: they could not tell
Which were birds and which was cloud.

A haunted silence held the tower,
Wherein the portrait's living eyes
Watched the dead lady with surprise,
Like a flower that gazes on a flower.

No doves returned there evermore.
The spiders wove about the door
Intricate tapestries of time,
That held the dew and held the rime.
And from the house of Colomen,
Like water from a frozen strand,
Failed the voices of maids and men,
Shrivelled the heart, shrivelled the hand,
Till there within the arching wood
No face was left but the painted face,
No sound was left of the human race,
But only the sound of doves that cooed
Sadly, intermittently –
Wheeling doves that none can see
But dying men who wander here
And see a picture, glassy-clear,
Where the milky hawthorn-blossom falls
And from the elm a blackbird calls:
Then softly from the ruined cote
A pigeon coos – and faint, remote,
A hundred pigeons answer low,
Voicing the lady's ancient woe;
And then they see her, very fair
And fragile in the scented air;
On arms and shoulders doves alight,
Multiple-tinted, like a bright
Tapestry that time has faded.
Softly purple, lilac-shaded,
The lady standeth, like a tree
Bent down with blossom. . . .

THE SPRING OF JOY

Vis Medicatrix Naturæ

Vis Medicatrix Naturæ

'We live the life of plants, the life of animals, the life of
men, and at last the life of spirits.'

SIR THOMAS BROWNE

ON some day of late January, when the honey-
coloured west is full of soft grey cloud, when one
lone minstrel thrush is chanting to the dying light, what
is the thrill that shakes us? It is not only that the delicate
traceries of silver birches are tenderly dark on the illumined sky, that a star springs out of it like darting quick-
silver, that the music of tone and tint has echoed last
April's song. It is something deeper than these. It is the
hidden sense – keen and startling – of oneness with all
beauty, seen and unseen. This sense is so misted over
that it only comes clearly at such times. When it does
come, we are in complete communion with the universal life. The winds are our playfellows; Sirius is our
fellow-traveller; we are swept up into the wild heart of
the wild. Then we know that we are not merely built
up physically out of flower, feather and light, but are
one with them in every fibre of our being. Then only
do we have our full share in the passion of life that fills
all nature; then only do we possess perfect vitality.
Then we are caught into the primal beauty of earth, and
life flows in upon us like an eagre. Life – the unknown
quantity, the guarded secret – circles from an infinite
ocean through all created things, and turns again to the
ocean. This miracle that we eternally question and
desire and adore dwells in the comet, in the heart of
a bird, and the flying dust of pollen. It glows upon

us from the blazing sun and from a little bush o
broom, unveiled and yet mysterious, guarded onl
by its own light – more impenetrable than dark
ness.

The power of this life, if men will open their heart
to it, will heal them, will create them anew, physicall
and spiritually. Here is the gospel of earth, ringin
with hope, like May mornings with bird-song, fresh an
healthy as fields of young grain. But those who woul
be healed must absorb it not only into their bodies i
daily food and warmth but into their minds, becaus
its spiritual power is more intense. It is not reasonabl
to suppose that an essence so divine and mysterious a
life can be confined to material things; therefore, if ou
bodies need to be in touch with it so do our mind
The joy of a spring day revives a man's spirit, reactin
healthily on the bone and the blood, just as the whol
some juices of plants cleanse the body, reacting on th
mind. Let us join in the abundant sacrament – for ou
bodies the crushed gold of harvest and ripe vin
clusters, for our souls the purple fruit of evening wit
its innumerable seed of stars.

We need no great gifts – the most ignorant of us ca
draw deep breaths of inspiration from the soil. Th
way is through love of beauty and reality, and throug
absorbed preoccupation with those signs of divinit
that are like faint, miraculous foot-prints across th
world. We need no passports in the freemasonry
earth as we do in the company of men; the only indi
pensable gifts are a humble mind and a receptiv
heart. We must go softly if we desire the butterfly

confidence; we must walk humbly if we dare to ask for an interpretation of this dream of God.

No accident of environment or circumstance need cut us off from Nature. Her spirit stirs the flowers in a town window-box, looks up from the eyes of a dog, sounds in the chirp of grimy city sparrows. From an observation hive in a London flat the bee passes out with the same dumb and unfathomable instinct that drove her from her home on Hybla of old. We may pry into her daily life, but her innermost secrets are as inviolable and as fascinating to us as they were to Virgil, watching from the beech-tree shade.

It does not matter how shut in we are. Opportunity or wide experience is of small account in this as in other things; it is depth that brings understanding and life. Dawn, seen through a sick woman's window, however narrow, pulses with the same fresh wonder as it does over the whole width of the sea. A branch of flushed wild-apple brings the same joy as the mauve trumpet-flower of the tropics. One violet is as sweet as an acre of them. And it often happens – as if by a kindly law of compensation – that those who have only one violet find the way through its narrow, purple gate into the land of God, while many who walk over dewy carpets of them do not so much as know that there is a land or a way.

The primal instincts can seldom be so dead that no pleasure or kinship wakens at the thronging of these vivid colours and mysterious sounds. Here is a kingdom of wonder and of secrecy into which we can step at will, where dwell nations whose very language is for-

ever unknown to us, whose laws are not our laws, y
with whom we have a bond, because we are anoth
expression of the life that created them. Here we fir
beauty that takes away the breath, romance that tingl
to the finger-tips. We think that there is some dee
meaning in it all, if we could only find it; sometimes w
catch an echo of it – in a plover's cry, in the silen
before a storm. So we listen, hearing a faint call fro
afar. It is this sense of mystery – unfading, because th
veil is never lifted – that gives glory to the countrysid
tenderness to atmosphere. It is this that sends one ma
to the wilds, another to dig a garden; that sings in
musician's brain; that inspires the pagan to build a
altar and the child to make a cowslip-ball. For in eac
of us is implanted the triune capacity for loving h
fellow and nature and the Creator of them. These love
may be latent, but they are there; and unless they an
all developed we cannot reach perfect manhood o
womanhood. For the complete character is that whic
is in communion with most sides of life – which see
hears, and feels most – which has for its fellows th
sympathy of understanding, for nature the love that
without entire comprehension, and for the myster
beyond them the inexhaustible desire which surel
prophesies fulfilment somewhere.

Earth is not only the mother of the young, the stron
the magnificent, whose tried muscles and long-limbe
grace are the embodiment of her physical life, in whos
eager glance burns the vitality of her spirit: she is als
the pitiful mother of those who have lost all; she wi
sing lullabies to them instead of battle-songs; she wi

pour her life into them through long blue days and silver nights; she will give back the mirth and beauty that have slipped through their fingers. When participation in man's keen life is denied, it is not strange if laughter dies. In the sirocco of pain it is not surprising if joy and faith are carried away. So many sit by the wayside begging, unconscious that the great Giver is continually passing down the highways and hedges of nature, where each weed is wonderful. So many are blind and hopeless, yet they have only to desire vision, and they will see that through His coming the thickets are quickened into leaf and touched with glory. Out in his world the spirit that was so desolate, lost in the strange atmosphere of physical inferiority, may once more feel the zest that he thought was gone for ever. And this zest is health: sweeping into the mind and into those recesses of being beyond the conscious self, it overflows into the body. Very often this great rush of joy, this drinking of the freshets of the divine, brings back perfect health. Even in diseases that are at present called incurable, and that are purely physical, no one will deny the immense alleviation resulting from this new life. It is possible that, as the spiritual ties between man and nature grow stronger, all disease may vanish before the vitality that will stream into us so swiftly, so easily, because it will not be confined to one channel. A man who holds direct intercourse with the cosmic life through his heart and mind knows a glad comradeship with cloud and tree; there dwells with him a consciousness of surrounding splendour – of swift currents, marvels underfoot and overhead; he has a purpose in waking each morning, a reason for existing – he clings to the beauty of earth as to a garment, and he feels that the wearer of the garment is God.

Beauty and Joy and Laughter are necessities of our being, and nature brims with them. There are some things that always bring joy – a ripple of song in winter, the blue flash of a kingfisher down-stream, a subtle scent that startles and waylays. The coming of spring brings it – the first crocus pricking up, dawn a moment earlier day by day, the mist of green on honeysuckle hedges in February, the early arabis, spicily warm, with the bees' hum about it. The flawless days of May bring it – when big white clouds sail leisurely over the sky, when the 'burning bush' is in the height of its beauty, and white lilac is out, and purple lilac is breaking from the bud, and chestnut spires are lengthening, and the hawthorn will not be long. Out in the fresh, green world, where thrushes sing so madly, the sweets of the morning are waiting to be gathered – more than enough for all, low at our feet, higher than we can reach, wide enough even for the travelling soul. Joy rushes in with the rain-washed air, when you fling the window wide to the dawn and lean out into the clear purity before the light, listening to the early 'chuck-chuck' of the blackbird, watching the pulse of colour beat higher in the east. Joy is your talisman when you slip out from the sleeping house, down wet and gleaming paths into the fields, where dense canopies of cobwebs are lightly swung from blade to blade of grass. Then the air is full of wings; birds fly in and out of the trees, scattering showers of raindrops as they dash from a leafy chestnut or disappear among the inner fastnesses of a fir. Pinions of dark and pinions of day share the sky, and over all are the brooding wings of unknown presences. The east burns; the hearts of the birds flame into music; the wild singing rises in a swelling rhythm until, as the first long line of light creeps across the meadows, the surging chorus seems to shake the treetops.

Laughter need not be lost to those that are cut off from their fellows. The little creatures of earth are the court jesters of all that dwell in the hall of sorrow. And although more insight and love are needed to enjoy their subtle humour than to enjoy our own, we have an ample reward of unfailing and spontaneous laughter. As vicarious grief is the keenest of all, so is vicarious laughter. Anyone who has watched the farcical solemnities of a rookery, the carefully thought-out inanities of wagtails, the drunken decorum of bees in full honey-flow, will not mind being cut off from human gatherings, where the laughter is sometimes a little mirthless. Anyone who has pondered on the ways of the meadow-ant – that influential dairy-farmer, with her prosperous herds of aphides, cared for with the same transparently self-interested devotion as the cottager's pig; and on the mind of the aphis – which allows itself to be milked and driven with such cowlike placidity; and on the hill-ants – who surreptitiously milk each other's cows – need never be dull.

There are many to whom all beauty seems denied; they hunger for it dumbly, unconsciously. Is their life to be a stricken tree, colourless and silent? Surely not.

It may be all illumined, like a sombre pine at the adven
of wood-pigeons – when there are low, contente
croonings instead of silence; soft, iridescent breast
against the harsh spines; widespread opal wings irra
diating the tree. The flawless forms and colours
nature are an especial consolation to those who ar
oppressed by that dark tragedy, deformity of body
unloveliness of face. How deep is the desolation, whe
a sad soul looks out anxiously, through eyes that canne
reflect its beauty, watching for an answering smile, an
meeting only a look of swiftly concealed repulsio
Startled and ill at ease in the ruinous mortal dwellin;
reminded of it continually, this soul leads a life
torture. I saw one of these look from her windows ar
weep bitterly, finding no comfort. Then a voice can
in the long sigh of the dawn breeze:

'I know, inhabitant of eternity, how strait and con
fortless your home is. Go out into my garden and fo
get. The skies are clear; see where I lead out my si
ereal flocks! The tall young larches are dreaming
green; there is moonlight in the primrose woo
There is a fit dwelling for you; go, and be at peac

She rose and went, and her laugh came back up
the wind. The leaves do not hesitate to finger and k
any face, however marred, that looks up into th
dwelling. No distortion of body frightens the birds,
the heart within loves them.

One flower of germander speedwell may be the ma
robe that clothes us with the beauty of earth. As t
maiden found her bridal garment in the fairy nut, so

may find in the folded speedwell-bud glimmering raiment to cover our homespun. It has the same strength of structure, wonder of tint and mystery of shadow as all natural things. Awakened by its minute perfection, the mind travels softly away through chequered woods, over the swinging sea, to mountains gleaming like a medieval paradise, forests of sumach, lakes of pink and blue lilies. Returning as from a trance, weary with splendour, it realizes that nature's beauty can never be perfectly grasped. Yet, since in essence it is the same wherever a blade of grass appears or a bird's shadow passes over; since the fact of seeing, in whatever degree, is the precious thing – let us go out along the lovely ways that lead from our doors into the heart of enchantment. Ceasing for a time to question and strive, let us dare to be merely receptive – stepping lightly over the dewy meadows, brushing no blue dust from the butterfly's wing. Then, if life is suddenly simplified by the removal of all that we hold most dear, we shall know the way to other things, not less precious. We shall know of long, green vistas, carpeted with speedwell, ascending to a place of comfort, and the blue butterfly will lead us into peace.

These three – Joy, Laughter, and Beauty – are the broadest river-ways down which may flow the essential life which itself is health and youth – beyond thought, beyond time, a sea that fills eternity – yet nearer than the air we breathe, immanent in the humblest creature, making material things transparent as a beech-leaf in the sun. And because those who most need its influx have only the least of earth's graces to watch, this book is concerned with muted skies, minute miracles, songs of the night, and the proud humility of the germ that holds in its littleness the Lord of Immortality.

Joy

The Joy of Motion

'My free soul may use her wing.'
GEORGE HERBERT

THE white grass-root – only a little blinder than the mole, a little less purposeful than the worm – goes softly about her dark house-cares in the close chambers where no wind comes, and sends out her sons with banners. When no breeze brushes the grass, we can very nearly see the multitudinous upward movement of the blades as they slip into the light in their ardent resurrection. When the trees are dumb on summer noons, we can almost hear the sap run. When no tread of man or beast disturbs the silence, we are haunted by the footsteps of the dust – of all those atoms that move invisibly and mysteriously to fresh unions for the building of hills and the hollowing of valleys. On such a day all the ripples of motion are in full flow; the tide of growth is coming in; all green things and flowers hold out their arms to the sun. In autumn the tide ebbs; leaf and petal look down to the soil whence they came as if they heard a call and longed to go back and inter-mingle with their kin; softly the petal flings herself down, and the leaf is not long in following. They go, not to death, but to a new incarnation among the unseen company that moves in silence, busier than a hive, creating daily a wonder greater than any myth – the world around us, with its mutable grace.

The story of any flower is not one of stillness, but of faint gradations of movement that we cannot see. The widening and lengthening of petals, the furling and unfurling of leaves, are too gentle for our uneducated eyes. The white convolvulus that flowers only for a day meets the early light folded as if with careful fingers, and dusk finds it folded in almost the same way. You would think that the stillness had never been broken; yet between dawn and twilight the flower's lifework has been completed in one series of smooth, delicate motions. The hour of the pointed bud has been followed by hours of change, until the time of the open blossom and the feeding bee; and even in that triumphant moment a faint tremor shook the spread corolla, and the final silent furling had begun. During the whole drama the flower has seemed stationary – like many spirits that grow from sheath to bud, open golden treasure and close again before our eyes – and we never see.

Watch a bank of periwinkle on an early summer morning. The fresh blue flowers are poised high on delicate stalks, and seem aloof from the leaves. Absolute stillness broods over them; no tremor is discernible in leaf or petal; the wide blue flowers gaze up intently into the wide blue sky. Suddenly, without any breath of wind, without so much stir as a passing gnat makes, one flower has left her stem. No decay touched her; it was just that in her gently progressive existence the time for erect receiving was over. Some faint vibration told her that the moment had come for her to leave off gazing stilly at the sky; and so, in silence and beauty, with soft precipitation, she buried her face in the enfolding evergreen leaves. This pale shadow of a gesture is as lovely, as inevitable, as the flight of wild swans beating up the sky.

In a glade carpeted with wood-sorrel, just before rain, you will be aware of something going on down among the frail companies of leaves. Returning after an absence of half an hour, you will see a difference in the look of every plant. Each triplet of leaflets has softly crinkled toward the stalk, umbrella-wise, and in another half-hour they will be all tightly clasped round it. It is startling to see such steady purpose in so small a plant.

Evening after evening, in the summer, I have gone to see the white clover fall asleep in the meadows. Kneeling and looking very closely, as the dew begins to gather, one sees a slight change in the leaves; all round the green is paler than by day – when the dark upper surfaces of the leaves are flat beneath the flowers – because the pale undersides are now visible. As the light fails, the two lower leaves on each stalk gently approach one another – like little hands that were going to clap, but thought better of it – and at last lie folded quietly, as if for prayer. Then the upper leaf droops, as a child's face might, until it rests on the others. Everywhere in the dusk the white clover leaves are sleeping in an attitude of worship; those who are early enough may see them wake and rise in the morning – multitudes moving in slow, unfaltering unity.

Unlike the clover, the wood-sorrel and the ivy-leaved toadflax move with sudden violence. The capsule of wood-sorrel opens with a jerk, flinging the seeds a long way in a seemingly erratic manner. The toadflax gives an impression of deliberate thought by the way its seed-vessel turns round on the stalk, seeking a suitable crevice on the wall where it grows, and then dropping the seeds in: it is difficult to distinguish the separate movements, because the flowers are small and crowded, and do not ripen all together.

The thought of this underlying agitation gives mystery to the more perceptible motions caused by the elements. One of the most captivating of these is the ripple of corn. It is so swift, so elusive, that the eye cannot follow it; it is a sea-dream to stand on a little hill and watch the whole countryside in delicious motion, furrowed by the invisible racing shallops of the breezes. The waves wash and break upon the flowery hedges and the remote horizon, and seem ready to submerge everything in their foamless flood. All solid things are made less solid by motion – so grass looks liquid, trees have an aerial magic when the wind is in them.

In summer the willows stroke the smooth water with their long fingers. The supple branches droop until they dip in the stream, and, as they sway, every thin leaf is followed by a vanishing hollow. One of the daintiest joys of spring is the falling of soft rain among blossoms. The shining and apparently weightless drops come pattering into the may-tree with a sound of soft laughter; one alights on a white petal with a little inaudible tap; then petal and raindrop fall together down the steeps of green and white, accompanied by troops of other petals, each with her attendant drop and her passing breath of scent. The leaves sit still and laugh, for they know that their time has not come, and the drops slide off shamefacedly and go elsewhere. The young buds laugh in their high places, strong in their immaturity; and all day the rain laughs among the thin, curved petals, till the descending drops are like silver wires from the treetop to the grass, and the petals slip down them like white beads.

How different from this spring lyric is the epic of autumn – a west wind in the wood! The leaves have lost their individuality, like a multitude of people on some calamitous day. Wild and reckless companies fly down the rides, beech and hornbeam, elm, ash and sycamore, in strangely assorted crowds – no longer in demure families, each on its own tree. The sound of their hurrying feet comes near, then with wild unreason they turn, desperately flying from the invisible. Before the old west wind that blows from the sunset, the wise wind that knew the Atlantic before a ship was on it, the strong wind that maddens the sea-horses, it is no wonder that the leaves are afraid. The very trees are bending double before it, groaning in the agony of their defiance. The lithe little birches sweep to earth in an ecstasy of surrender; the fir-trees lash themselves; the saplings have learnt obedience – their slender elasticity is at the wind's will; only the stiff old oaks and elms refuse to yield, and ominous crashes tell of their struggle. The live creatures of the wood have hidden from the tumult. The most living things in the place are the leaves; with their scurrying feet and their complaining, whispering voices, they are like an elfin nation, a lost tribe, a defeated army that has forgotten discipline. The sight and the sound of this world-old conflict brings the same strong exhilaration as music does, when it quickens and deepens to a climax.

What new and romantic discoveries await the explorer in the pilgrimages of animals! Mysterious journeyings of fox, badger, weasel and rat; the nomadism of frogs and eels; migrations of those 'water-swallows,' the trout; ocean wanderings of the oleander hawk-moth, who, for all her frailty, will venture hundreds of miles from land – these movements, of which we know so little, are not mere restlessness, but planned and ordered comings and goings. We often have one glimpse of them – a weasel runs across a lane from spinney to spinney; a water-rat scurries past upon an unknown errand; a rabbit comes up from his hole upon pressing business and scampers off into obscurity; or a shy little field-mouse creeps from her nest and goes back in a flurry. Most of us have to be content with this, for not many have the unique qualities necessary for watching the free and secret lives of the wild creatures. It is even more difficult to be intimate with birds, for with a flash of wings they are gone in an instant beyond all clues. With migratory birds especially, mystery is the chief part of the story.

All summer you watch a pair of swallows; you seem to be getting to know them, to be nearer their secret. Then a day comes when the aspens are beginning to be flecked with gold, long sprays of yellow tansy sweep the water, and in the hearts of the fruited elder-bushes are faint twitterings and gentle flutterings. Looking down into the golden-tinted stream you see far within it the shadows of your swallows, remote and vague, as if the mist of distance had already descended between you and them, and you know that soon they will be only birds of memory, mere flashes of the past, instead of the intimate little friends of your summer days. You can never know to what sun-baked cornice, what warm blue pool or purple-fruited tree they went on those swift wings of theirs. The passage of two birds across the sky appeals indescribably to the imagination. They come from the farthest horizon, flying swiftly high in the blue, pursuing their intent way and vanishing — you know not whither. They go to some far trysting-place, some nest that is to be in willow or darkling fir, some place that their ancestors have known; and we are left with a memory of wings dividing the air and a sense of frustration.

The coming of a dipper up-stream is worth watching for all a summer day. Suddenly, at a far bend, in the green dimness of overarching trees, there is a flash of white. Like a fairy shield, it comes on steadfastly through shadow and sunlight with a smooth and gliding motion, growing larger and larger until the last bright piece of water is traversed on still, outspread wings, and the bird alights gently on a stone.

Few things are more stimulating than the sight of the forceful wings of large birds cleaving the vagueness of air and making the piled clouds a mere background for their concentrated life. The peregrine falcon, be-calmed in the blue depths, cruises across space without a tremor of his wide wings. Wild geese beat up the sky in a compact wedge. Primeval force is in their strongly-moving wings and their beautiful, outstretched necks, in their power of untiring effort, and the eager search of their wild hearts for the free spaces they love. The good-fellowship of swift, united action, the joy of ten thousand that move as one, is in the flight of flocks of birds. When sea-gulls flash up from the water with every wing at full stretch there is no deliberation; it is as if each bird saw a sweeping arc before it and followed its individual way faithfully. The unerring judgment of the grand curve when the wings are so near and yet never collide, the speed of the descent, are pure poetry.

In the dipping flight of little birds, such as sparrows, linnets and tits, there is something reminiscent of cup and ball – a very light ball in a very large cup. The bird sinks in the air and is gently tossed up again, dipping continually; yet it flies with arrowy speed. The enthusiasm of the process, the buoyancy of the little thing which can afford to spend so much more strength than it needs, make it an incarnation of youth and gaiety.

In spring the wood-pigeon forgets fleet-winged adventure, and flutters, tethered – for he has a treasure. Then, too, the greenfinch is overtaken by happy languor, and falters in her flight, smitten with the April madness.

Bees' wings moving give a sense of absolute ease because the energy seems so great in proportion to the frail weight lifted. It is restful to watch these creatures so ethereal of body, so abundantly gifted with vitality – young gnats, the daintiest of dancers, ephemeral and swift, with their tireless measure – hive bees, standing round their doors on a hot day, their thin, airy wings flickering fast, making a cool stir with their noiseless rhythm. Even the great dor-beetles and fluffy bumble-bees – those angry people of the fields – fling their stout bodies through the air with a careless ease that implies immense reserves of power. The dragon-fly, fiery with purposeful energy, flashes over the stream in some long quest, like Palomides. Those small electric-blue insects, that make a haze over water-meadows in June, continue their innumerable dartings briskly in the most swooning heat; but there is nothing brisk in the opening and folding of a butterfly's wings; they are softly and weightlessly sleepy. She comes along the golden day with her faint, continual flutter; her wings make a gentle vibration in the air; from far down the stretches of ripe, brown grass-meadow you watch her approach, and because of her the place becomes Elysium. The white moth's passing is a lullaby; her wings have the elusiveness of dreams as she flickers down the dusk and alights contentedly upon the opening campion.

Movements of which we become conscious through one sense alone bring a strange feeling of secrecy. Owls' flight and all other motions of which we should know nothing with our eyes shut, have an eeriness because of this purposeful quiet; it is uncanny that the strength of those swooping wings should be so utterly noiseless. In a lightning flash, coming in the deep hush after thunder, lies terror; such unthinkably swift and formless motion, instantaneously bridging the abyss of space without a sound, is like some fearful portent. Are our senses undeveloped, since the dramas of dawn and moonrise have for us no chorus; the wind steals by invisible; the stars go through their stately ritual with silent tread, weaving their radiant dances to no murmur of music?

Unseen activity hints of imminent, ungauged power. Isaiah's idea of communion with the Deity was clothed in terms expressing invisible motion. Any stir of life is ominous if we cannot see it, because we are left uncertain as to the strength behind it; rustling in a wood on a moonless night may be caused by slight or overwhelming forces. So it is with the wind – that bodiless voice crying in the great spaces of the air, shouting round our roofs and chimneys, sighing at our windows, yelling above the passion of a storm at sea, fluting in the summer treetops. It is like a whisper in the night, when you cannot tell whether a child or a man is speaking; like some creature flapping at our doors in the gloom. We never see the gates of its dark house swing open, nor watch it fall beyond the waters into its tomb beneath the yellow sunset. Every day since the earth was, the wind has sighed and sung around it, gathering up the laughter and tears of all creatures and taking them into its ageless liberty. More mysterious than the invisible wind is the wind that is simply felt, blowing where there are no trees in which to watch it, pressing upon one with tireless, invincible force. There are few things that bring such awe and delight; for it is stronger than a thousand strong horses, shadowless and secret as a god.

Nature sets her dances to every rhythm, from slow undulations to the swift, dangerous rushes that bring wild exhilaration. The long pendulum-swing of trees is restful, not in the unambitious manner of quiescence — that might mean death; nor with a sudden cessation of movement — that might mean injury; but with the content of a return after swaying out from a fixed place, which implies balance and vitality. In the same way a poised mind sweeps out to all new ideas, but is not torn from its place because of its roots.

In this world of swinging, swaying, cleaving, fluttering motion, what is the part of the man who is obliged to be still? It is in his eager mind. Looking from the drowsy room, which is the world of his body, into the stirring life outside, he who longs for the gay kindliness of comradely exertion can project himself into the glad errantries of nature. He can gallop on the wild horses of wave and wind, outspanning his team in the caravanserai of night. He can pass with the stars on their long marches. He can peer through the soil with growing grass and slip in and out of wet spring coverts with nesting birds. As the doors into physical busyness are shut, more may be opened into the lusty activities of the spirit; and through these doors are vistas of fresh joy — it overflows the very sills like ground ivy. Those who have complete bodily freedom will probably never enter fully into the deep happiness brought by waving grass and running water: but he who has time and who cares to use his imagination, can see in all natural things the bowing down of the creature before the Creator. Perhaps a young larch grows near his window, and he loves the strong, elastic swing of the branches. Or he may have a company of Lombardy poplars to watch, and can see them, when he lies awake on a windy night, catching the stars in their green meshes with a sweep like that of a butterfly net. Possibly he can see nothing but sky. Then he can observe uninterruptedly the speed of grey March clouds before their sheep-dog, the gale; the shepherding of white midsummer flocks toward evening; the massing of them for thunder. The advent of the first star, the swimming rose of dawn passing up the sky, the sun's progress in lonely majesty through the great hollow heaven of summer, will mean more to him than to other people. A watcher of the melodic ritual of earth cannot know stagnation of soul; his ideas are fresh and vigorous. Although the healthy quickening of the pulse after exertion, the joy of hard work, may be denied to a man, adventures of the soul are his, along 'the way that no fowl knoweth.' Who can say that such enterprises of an eager spirit may not be nearer to real life – the life of the unknown forces that hold the wandering star and guide the travelling moon – than are the more comprehensible adventures of the body?

'A gift was given to Brother Bernard of Quintavalle, to wit, that he fled flying like the swallows.'

The Joy of Music

'Eftsoons they heard a most melodious sound.'

SPENSER

THE music of nature, vocal and orchestral, laughs and sobs through the seasons with eternal variations. Ominous, reassuring, triumphant, tender, it swells across the world and across the ages in majestic diapason, and is suddenly hushed for the humble solo of a robin. The composition is so large and intricate that we cannot discern the thread of the melody nor the idea beneath the music. Sometimes we distinguish a few chords, even a bar or two; but our grasp is too small and our life too short to attain any continuous consciousness of its development. We are like people who come into an opera house and hear a snatch of some bridal song or a stave of the Pilgrims' Chorus, and then are called away. Occasionally some of the detached sounds weave themselves into an air. I have heard rain on leaves, the lowing of cattle, and the shrill song of a gnat unite in this way. But as a rule we have to be content with scattered and lonely notes – like one who knows some distant music only through the floating echo of a flute, the far, sweet quiver of a violin. This music has for treble the faint cheeping of little birds, the falling of a seed, the flow of sap; for bass the loud utterances of the sea, the passion and melancholy of the winds.

Some notes bring more joy than others, perhaps because they mean more. When the first thrush sings between January snowstorms with such appealing charm, he is chanting the recitative that leads on the great spring chorus. Something like his must have been the song of the first bird on the earliest budding tree when the world was young. Akin to it may be the song of some early-waking spirit (and who can say that spirits shall not awake, like the scarlet moth from her chrysalis, the golden bird from her egg?) beginning falteringly the music that will be taken up – like the chant of a dawn blackbird – by the gathering glee-men.

How the thrush sings in April on the high yew-bough! You may stand close to his tree and watch his bright throat quiver; he is so absorbed that he never hears a footstep. How thrillingly he pleads:

'Come hither, love, come here, come here to me!
Now, now, now, now! Come to the yew-tree bough!
Sweet dear! *Sweet* dear! Mine! Mine!
Come, or I come to you – you – you!
Come here, come here to me!'

He sings in the air as he flies; he sings on the ground; he is afire with song. Among the pale green elm samaras the blackbird sits alone, and out of his long brooding weaves a strong enchantment. He sings, falls in his effortless way from the green height to the green depth, and sings again.

Now in every country place the birds translate their happiness into delicious song. 'Live! Laugh!' cries the chiff-chaff all day long, careless of elaboration if he can give his message, effectually cutting the silence with his two small notes like silver shears. The tom-tit, with characteristic egotism, shouts 'Me, me, me!' The yellow-hammer and the hedge-sparrow tell over their short, recurring staves. The green linnet sits erect, though his body sways with music; the notes come slipping through the leaves like rain, and sometimes he throws back his head and laughs. The cheery babble of starlings fills any pauses, and the lark – Mercury of spring – goes on skyey messages. Then one morning you wake to a consciousness of something more; across the lighter singing strikes the bourdon note of the cuckoo, expressing the cosmos for himself in two syllables, saying the same thing as cuckoos were saying when Watling Street was made, of which we long to know the interpretation. The willow wrens begin their ethereal whisperings; the blackcap comes. He is the meistersinger of gardens where the nightingale is absent; in a moment, as you stand by the willow where he is, he opens the doors of delight. His swift, winning phrases go lilting up and down in continuous sweetness for an hour at a time. Then suddenly there are the swallows, clinging to the eaves and to branches over water, chattering with lovely monotony, singing long songs that pass and come again – low, serene, contemplative. So all day between dusk and dusk there is music, and even in the dark the sedge warbler wakes and sings. While night pales toward the dawn, you can hear him down in the dim trees by the water; his tenuous notes are scarcely strong enough to pierce even the silence, but to sleepless people weary of the night his song is comfortable. They love him for singing his

153

lonely, small roundelay, not waiting for the chorus or the sun.

Multitudes of soft sounds make up the music of spring – a gentle stir of growth, the crisp rustle of daffodils against one another, the wind communing with young leaves; and the air is full of plaintive voices of small creatures questioning of life. As the grass grows deep, and June slips by, the birds sing only in the cool, and the burden of the music is taken up by the trees and the fields. When the ear is attuned to this fainter singing, it hears in each tree a different voice, sighing, discoursing, laughing. Oak leaves, on their firm, stiff stems, brush one another roughly; long, pendent willow leaves move with a sleepy whisper; chestnut leaves lip one another consolingly. Aspens and poplars have their leaves hung loosely on stalks almost as flexible as the veins; they are soft and thick, so the mere hint of a breeze sets them twisting round to talk together; the continual motion sounds like running water, and in a quiet place you can hear it across a wide field. The wind fans in the maple, harps in the needles of a pine, sighs in silver birches, and rolls like an organ in the cedar.

The other chief singer of summer is the grass; it is the very voice of Earth, taking us into her confidence. To hear it you must go to some upland, away from water and trees, and lie with the green forest above you. Then you will hear the silky ripple of the blades and the velvet caress of the ripe, brown grass-heads, swelling to a multitudinous soft whisper as the breeze goes

154

by. These murmurs, the hum of bees in the clover, the shrilling of crickets, charm and possess the silent noon. Falling into a dream you will suddenly be startled by a resonant, imperious voice close by, shouting in a strange language. Rising on your elbow, mystified, you will see a small dark bird running away among the grass; and for once you will have heard the corncrake as the little people of the fields hear him.

Of all summer music there is nothing more contented than the sound of a herd cropping cool grass in the shade; it is as refreshing to hear as running water. When the cows come farmwards at milking time with the unyoked horses, a harmonious tumult rises, filling the warm silence as syllabub fills a bowl. Among all these gentle melodies there breaks out the occasional forceful bass of a thunderstorm, with rushes of rain and an eerie wind which passes furtively in the tree-tops.

Just before autumn the oat fields begin their dry-throated song, louder than that of the grass, and the heavier grains keep time with fairy castanets. Sounds of reaping begin to haunt the air; the prelude of autumn has begun. On still, September mornings, when a sweet warm wind blows under the grey sky, sounds carry far – the bleating of sheep, calls from far-off fields, the sharp trot of a horse on a hard road, the hum of threshing. The rooks fly in a long black thread across the uplands to the stubble-fields, and the sense of tranquillity is deepened by their erratic cawing. Some of the harshest tones of nature bring the deepest rest.

Few things are so unmusical as the voices of rooks, yet a home with a rookery is a very peaceful place. Perhaps the continual cawing, like the ticking of a clock in a quiet room, emphasizes the surrounding hush; perhaps it is the associations of childhood and calm days; or is it something deep and old as earth that lurks in the harsh voices and comes poignantly to our hearts? Hear them on a windless evening, winging homeward heavily through the rain, with desultory cawing! Listen as they settle clamorously for the night and you will know how well they fill the pauses made by departing sweetness.

Autumn is full of leave-taking. In September the swallows are chattering of destination and departure like a crowd of tourists, and soon they are gone. Gone also are the willow wrens and the blackcaps and the reed sparrows, and the cuckoo has long been part of the echoing past. It is the day of small things; the wren's bell-like note and the wild little song of the tits are quite impressive now. The robin is chief singer; his voice ascends like a spiral stair, every ringing note a roundel for the mounting spirit. Down through the sere leaves comes the first chestnut; others follow in quickening commotion, beginning their long pilgrimage to perfection; a hundred years hence they will stand in bridal white against the blue. Then the complaint of falling leaves begins, swells in a ghostly crescendo, and is hushed. Once more, as in early spring, the air is full of wings; missel thrushes, fieldfares and redpolls are busy in the ploughlands; great gatherings of starlings assemble in the afternoon to go to roost in the reeds when thousands of them rise together, there is a sound like the unfurling of a silken banner. Flocks of wild geese pass over, and their strange cry falls from the sky. The peewits wheel and call continually, and from amid the ripple of their wings their cry sounds ost and lovely as some Naiad's voice beneath running water.

Now the four winds stand up to sing their winter song – the melancholy south, the east, inarticulate with mist, the wild west, and the sonorous north with its half-audible sigh of snow. Their strong, masculine voices harmonize perfectly with the severe outline of winter. The thud of snow from creaking pine-branches, the cracking of ice on the meres, the reverberating fall of rocks split by the black frost on the hilltop, the shivering whimper of owls – these are the crude notes of the dark months.

So the year's music draws to the close which means a new beginning. In listening to it there is never the unrest that one feels in hearing a beautiful song – the sorrow of knowing that it will soon be over. Nature's music is never over; her silences are pauses, not conclusions. They emphasize the music. It is between thunderclaps, when the reverberations have sunk into dense stillness, that you realize the thunder. When you lean from your window into the silence of a country night you are not aware of it at first. It is like an invisible, enclosing bowl, and you become aware of its depth only when a fox's bark rings in, like a sharp silver thing striking the sides once and yet again, or when the song of a willow

157

wren patters into it in a succession of liquid notes. Few things bring such healing to a worn spirit as this silence, which falls softly, layer upon layer on the jaded mind, like blossom on a rough cart track.

Music expresses the other delights of nature and is intensified by them. So the calling of cuckoos completes the beauty of the grass fields – racing shadows, depths of green powdered with daisies, the scent of vernal grass, are all taken up into the haunting cry. So the blackbird gives to all the silent breaths and pulses of April a voice, and they give him a setting for his song. When the wych-elm sprays are crimson rosaries, set and ordered without fingers; when the pear trees are hung with bright little globes that shine like rain-drops, and are indeed drops from the great storm of life that is sweeping over all things – then the rhapsody of a blackbird says for us all the things that we feel. His is a magic melody, sweeter even than the singing of those wondrous birds of Rhiannon, whose song 'was at a great distance over the sea, yet appeared as distinct as if they were close by. And fourscore years passed as a day in listening to them, and there was no remembrance of sorrow whatsoever.' In every field are more magical songs than these; fourscore Aprils seem a very little time to spend in listening; and while you are in the charmed circle – though your eyes may be full of tears – there is no remembrance of sorrow at all.

Sometimes, when the music of earth is most arresting, we seem to hear through it an unknown personality, far off in the terror of great beauty, summoning us poor wanderers in tones reassuring as a herdsman's call to his cattle on the mountains – simple and homely.

The Joy of Fragrance

'Chests of fragrant medicinal balm
To work cool ointments for the grievèd flesh.'

CHARLES WELLS

AS the colour-blind slowly learn to distinguish
shades of blue and green, so the scent-clogged may
explore the almost unknown delight of fragrance, until
they can disentangle the ravelled sweetness in the air. We
know by the colour of her burden under what friendly
roof the bee asked alms this morning – whether she
begged in the brown hut of the figwort or the rosy
pavilion of the willow herb. So when the wind comes
along secret ways with the laugh of a naughty child who
has found a treasure and will not tell of it, we know where
he has been by the scents that cling to him like burrs to
a truant lad. Here are the sharpness of bilberry leaves,
the emanation of moss, the reek of a blue-spired bon-
fire, the resin of sticky poplar buds, the metheglin of
white violets, and somewhere among them lingers the
keenness of spray from the home of sea-mews.

Sometimes, when the east wind is full of meditative
savagery, one almost fancies that a hot odour may have
travelled in its caravan from the heart of China, bringing us a message from the spice trees of Kwang-
tung.

As in some uncanny flowers and distorted trees there
seems to be an evil influence, so in many cloying scents
there is sorcery. Down where the pale turf is dank
among the harsh smells of yew-trees, laurels, and Herb
Paris, one almost sees the malevolent fair face of Vivian

160

as she passes – delicate and dishevelled – among the tangled shadows, weaving incantations with her wimple. Crush the purple orchis or berries of black bryony, and their necromancy brings dim thoughts of evil schemings, dishonoured deaths, unholy rites. Then gather a spray of wild artemisia; its sweet influence will exorcise the sense of brooding harm; it brings remembrance of well-being and well-doing, of love triumphant and dreams come true. When the honeyed wine of apple blossom is in the air and the freshness of dew is like a caress, we hear the youth of the world laughing – we see Perdita with her arms full of daffodils, and Atalanta coming through the meadows with wet, white feet.

These immemorial essences fill the mind with purple haze and auroral mist, conjuring impalpable visions of ancient things.

The origin of flower scents is full of mystery. Sometimes they seem to run through the minute veins like an ichor, as in wallflowers, with their scented petals; sometimes they are locked in the pollen casket, or brim the nectar-cup; sometimes they come from the leaf-pores, as in balm, and sometimes from the roots in addition, as in primroses and lilies. The essence lies in the arms of that small creature, the seed, who seldom tells her secret.

Flowers like the oxlip, with transparently thin petals, only faintly washed with colour, yet have a distinct and pervasive scent. Daisies are redolent of babyhood and whiteness. Wood anemones, lady's smock, bird's-foot trefoil and other frail flowers will permeate a room with their fresh breath. In some deep lane one is suddenly pierced to the heart by the sweetness of woodruff, inhabitant of hidden places, shining like a little lamp on a table of green leaves. It is like heliotrope and new-mown hay with something wholly individual as well. To stand still, letting cheek and heart be gently buffeted by the purity, is to be shriven.

The violet has long had such poor, negative virtues as modesty and self-effacement ascribed to her, because she stays in her hidden nook, apparently a very humble and unknown little creature. But from her quiet haunt she sends forth her fragrance like a voice into the world – the expression of a soul so rich that it cannot be contained within her narrow dwelling. She impresses it upon the gale; the wind becomes her henchman and carries it upon his shoulders. Then such as love violets travel up the strengthening sweetness and find this sleeping beauty in her fastness, tearing their hands and healing their hearts. So she finds her worshippers, her lovers.

Many common flowers have the graciousness of personality that some rare women have. Agrimony is one of these. Walking along a dusty highway in July, one becomes aware that every breath is a blessing from some wayside flower; and tracing the resinous sweetness as it freshens through the dust, finds the hitherto unnoticed spike of little yellow stars. Those who go by a wood in May are enfolded in a wave of delight, and whispering 'Wild hyacinths!' feel as if a child had kissed them.

Fragrance is the voice of inanimate things. The air

is full of the cries of leaves and grass, softer than those of the flowers. In the dark night of the cedar there is a different atmosphere from that within the dusk of beeches or the green gloom of April larch woods. Sometimes, in places where there are no flowers, aromas dart upon one like little elves with sharp teeth, from corn and fir-cones, damp soil and toadstools, keen grass and pungent bracken. Even rock sends out a curious redolence in hot weather which unites with dried ling and herbs to form an undercurrent to the mellowness of gorse.

Down by a stream at dusk the water takes up into its freshness the breath of mallow, pennyroyal and willow-herb as they sway in their sleep. In a shower, unsuspected sweets rush out of ambush with a laugh, overpowering and imprisoning us. In the dewy summer dark, clover and night-flowering stock conspire with the campion and the sleepless honeysuckle to invade the drenched garden and to conquer and possess the dreaming house.

Often in winter across leagues of snow a mysterious fragrance comes, inexplicable until we remember that snow itself has a faint emanation, and that the essence of pines, of last year's hay and far-off violets can wander across the pure air for long distances, treasured (like wine in a crystal glass) by the frost.

Is anyone sickened by the sordidness of life? Let him go to the tents of flowering trees, when the cavalcade of the wild bee comes to the apple as the Arabs to Mecca, when the spinneys are fresh with quicken, and the fly hovers like a lover outside the shut door of the pear blossom and waits till the red cross of denial that marks the bud is changed to the yellow pollen-wreath of fulfilment.

The fragrance of limes, when every honey-dripping tassel has its clinging bee, is like the hail of a friend. The poignancy of it and the deep note of the bees weave themselves into a circumambient peace, within which each tree dwells like Saturn in his rings. It is fainter in the outer precincts, deepening to such a breathless delight as one penetrates to the centre that it is difficult to remember which sense is in touch with the voice of the bees and which with the voice of the tree.

A little wood I know has in May among its oaks and beeches many white pillars of gean trees, each with its own air round it. At long intervals a large, soft flower wanders down, vaguely honeyed, mixing its breath with the savour of sphagnum moss, and resting among the wood-sorrel. The wood-pigeons speak of love together in their deep voices, unashamed, too sensuous to be anything but pure. Among the enchanted pillars, on the carpet of pale sorrel, with a single flower cool in the hand, one is in the very throne-room of white light. A little further on the air is musky from the crowded minarets of the horse chestnut – white marble splashed with rose – where the bumble bee drones.

Insects are the artists of fragrance; they have a genius for it; there seems to be some affinity between the tenuity of their being and this most refined of the sense-impressions. Ghostly calls summon them to their banquets. The crane's-bill has a word for the gnat; the helleborine fills her goblet only for the wasp; the yellow iris calls to the honey-fly; the meadow saffron's veined cup is for the bee. Moths call each other by scent; so do bees; and probably the smallest ephemera follow the same law. These calls and answers cross the world continually, like a web of fine threads, most of them too slight for our comprehension.

Nature spreads her sweets for the poor: she gives them rosemary instead of sandal-buds, wild cassia instead of cinnamon, iris roots and ploughman's spikenard for those who cannot buy attar of roses. The nectar of full hives, warm wax, dry leaves, ripening apples – these are her commonplaces. The very beetle climbing a rough willow is redolent of flowers. On the darkest day of the year, with sleet in the air, you can find in the sombre shelter of a yew tree a pale blossom scented like heliotrope. It is only the wild butterbur, yet its delicacy lifts the wintry day on to the steps of summer. Among the most desolate sandhills you may find in July acres of wax-white pyrola – like lilies of the valley splashed with pink – covering the plains between the lonely ridges of harsh, grey grass. The forlorn sigh of the grass is drowned by the humming of bees over the glistening carpet, and from every flower rises an intense fragrance.

The whole earth is a thurible heaped with incense, afire with the divine, yet not consumed. This is the most spiritual of earth's joys – too subtle for analysis, mysteriously connected with light and with whiteness, for white flowers are sweetest – yet it penetrates the physical being to its depths. Here is a symbol of the material value of spiritual things. If we washed our souls in these healing perfumes as often as we wash our hands, our lives would be infinitely more wholesome. The old herbalists were wise in their simplicity in the making of marigold potions, medicaments of herbs, soothing unguents from melilot and musk-mallow, elecampane and agrimony, pillows for the sick from rosemary and basil, beech-leaf mattresses for the weary – for these things cleanse the whole being. 'Golden saxifrage for melancholy, blue vervain for working magic cures,' said the old physicians; and still the shining saxifrage shames the discontented, and the rare blue vervain diffuses magic. The pasque-flower – dark purple, sun-hearted, with its symbolism of the old grief and the young joy that the Christian mystic puts into the word Easter – was given for cataract: it cures a darkness worse than that of the eyes. The Arabs give a fusion of roses for phthisis; the aconite, under her cold, slaty roof, keeps a simple for fevers; from the pink cistus, with its heart of five flames, comes the merciful labdanum. Such things are a cordial for body and soul.

A thousand homely plants send out their oils and resins from the still places where they are in touch with vast forces, to heal men of their foulness. They link the places that humanity has made so chokingly dusty with the life-giving airs of the ambrosial meadows – bringing women's heads round quickly and setting people smiling.

166

Not once only, but every year, the fair young body of the wild rose hangs upon the thorn, redeeming us through wonder, and crying across the fetid haunts of the money-grubbers with volatile sweetness – 'Father . . . they know not what they do.'

Laughter

Laughter

'Come live, and be merry, and join with me,
To sing the sweet chorus of "Ha, ha, he!"'

WILLIAM BLAKE

THERE is a path that leads from every one's door into the country of young laughter: but you must stoop to find it. The branches laugh and sigh above; willow-herb and traveller's joy cover you with their soft fleeces; fennel and flowering mint make the air spicy; the burdock and the bedstraw stretch out their hands to catch you. There the birds sit so erectly prim and so silently mirthful that you often have to clap your hand over your mouth like a child in case your echoing laughter should disturb the place. When you have gone a little way, the path may end without warning in a rabbit burrow, or the dome of a mole's winter palace, or the hanging cradle of a long-tailed tit. Then back you must go and begin again, only to come to a standstill soon before the frail barrier of a spider's web, swung from opposite thorn trees. Nothing must be broken here, or you find yourself left in a grey world, with all the irresponsible gaiety of the enchanted pathway folded in stiff sadness like a dead moth's wing.

The first time I went there was in May. Across the way hung a hollow ivy-bush, through which ran a long branch of wild apple. Inside the bush, absurdly crowded together half-way along the bough, were six very young and very small long-tailed tits. How they could be out in the world at all was amazing. They were not in the least dismayed. They gazed at me unblinkingly in the dignity of their long tails, with un-ruffled equanimity. Suddenly it seemed to me that those minute balls of fluff were my self-constituted judges. I was constrained to whisper – very softly for fear of frightening them – 'Not guilty, my lords!' Then I fled up the path to have my laugh out, and returned in a little while to find the court empty, their lordships having adjourned. In some miraculous manner they had been spirited away by their parents, and I could never find them again; so the verdict remains unknown to me.

Later in the year I went further down the path to a place where a crowd of young bullfinches were eating dandelion seeds. They hung on to the flower-heads in an incompetent way, like inexperienced and rather stout trapeze performers, and the elastic stalks bent with them so that they bobbed up and down continually with their energy. Beside a gate from which a lamb with a musical forehead and a stentorian voice observed them, some young chaffinches and greenfinches were playing in a minute pool of rainwater left from a thunderstorm. The idea had just come to them that they must wash; so in they fluttered, and flicked a few drops over their chests. They were so like children paddling, that I said, 'Children, children, wet your fore-heads!' – and immediately the air was full of little wings and flying drops of water. Looking back, I saw them sitting gravely along a low larch bough, cogitating. They were wondering about the new sound in their quiet world, and as they are rather slow-witted little birds, very likely they are wondering still. Are these hings childish? Then it is good to be childish: there is something in the atmosphere of the fennel-path that purifies the heart.

On a certain day in autumn, when the herbs on either side were more pungently sweet because a frost had touched them, when the first winter violet appeared among its fresh leaves, a young thrush, stirred by some fragrance as of spring in the warm day, instinctively began to sing. But he did not know a song! He reasoned with himself doubtfully, tentatively, among the golden columns of the trees that upheld the low, grey sky; but no inspiration came to him; he was unready, as yet, for his true song – sure, unwavering, recklessly glad. There was sadness in the mellow morning, pathos in the low notes, because the trees must feel weights of snow and the thrush taste the bitterness of winter before the young leaves and the ecstatic song could spring up together into the light. On a chestnut bough, already bare, a young blackbird was shouting a stave. He had probably remembered quite suddenly the golden roundelay his father sang when *he* was only a quick-breathing bundle in the nest. With the touching hopefulness and arrogance of youth he thought he could sing it then and there. So he rushed into self-expression, and produced something faintly resembling the full, round call, but with a very humiliating rasp at the end. Misgiving crept into his soul, but he was determined, he went on; and his sisters, humbly perched upon a lower bough, listened with rapt admiration – for they, poor things, could not sing a note. The same quaint mixture of a laugh and a sigh comes when you hear a starling at his orisons. It is such a funny little hymn, and it trails off so queerly into a kind of – 'I wonder whatever I can say next!' But he sings with uplifted head and quick spreadings of his wings, and though he is ludicrous, his earnestness is lovable. His song is not much, but it is his best.

One winter day the path led me to a hall of pine-trunks, where I watched a nut-hatch go up an aspen tree. He was a solemn bird; he had a look of concealed scorn when his eye rested on anything that was not a nuthatch. I sat down .to see which of us would be obliged to give way to merriment first, and the nut-hatch won. He went on, laboriously creeping round and round, tapping absorbedly, looking down occasionally, as if to see whether I had been dazzled by his shining example and was also beginning to creep and tap. He did not care whether I laughed or not; he simply hammered. I longed to ask him whether he agreed with the maxim that genius is the infinite capacity for taking pains; but of course he does. Equally persevering is the dipper, with his knee-strengthening exercises; were we dippers, we think, having the freedom of those translucent green waterways, we would not stand on a hot stone, exercising for half the day. Yet the dipper is very like some of us. So is the bumble-bee, paying a house-to-house visitation among the nasturtiums, saying in her thick voice, 'Most important – help urgently needed! Hunger in the nest – great mortality among the young bees!' As she goes off laden one is almost sure that a demure ripple of laughter passes over the arch nasturtiums. The robin, revelling n detail, chirping platitudinously, is Polonius to the ife. As he surveys you, head awry, you hear – 'That he s mad, 'tis true: 'tis true, 'tis pity: and pity 'tis, 'tis rue.' He has just the lisp to say it well. This is only n the summer: later, he gets him a soul and a song. The sparrow, like all street singers, sounds his scrannel note with raucous complacency; but it does not matter here, for no one is critical or talks of Art.

Once, on a July morning, I ran through the corn-flower-blue shadows of the path to a grove of young ir-trees, and was present at a breakfast party given by he willow warblers. A good many chiff-chaffs and wood wrens were there; they seemed to be vivaciously discussing last winter's African adventures. They had nvited the tomtits. 'Poor things,' one can imagine hem saying, 'they are so provincial; it will widen their minds.' The conversation being so cosmopolitan, the its were rather quiet and ruffled of crest. After about an hour the warblers began to sing, the tomtits helping, making up for the fewness of their notes by shouting at he tops of their voices. It must have been a kind of grace, for afterwards they all flew away. Some ducks n a pond close by were cackling with laughter; down vent their heads among the water-lilies, and every time hey righted themselves they shrieked again. In the centre sat one duck who neither dived nor shouted, but quacked monotonously, as if she were saying – 'O my isters, life is very solemn.' Through all her utterances he others continued to stand on their heads and shriek hysterically, as if they knew that her kill-joy attitude vas not really high principle, but adipose deposit.

Further on, in a still, hot place, a company of Red Admiral butterflies drank sap on a big tree trunk, and a peacock butterfly was resting, fanning her wings.

Often I have walked in the fennel path all day, watching the gay life there, where the birds sit each in a mist of song and the squirrel indulges in graceful buffoonery. In the ploughlands on either side the plovers gravely go through their one trick every year, tempting the pursuer from their nest with mock fear and inward satisfaction. There the inconsequent stream that runs beside the path, bearing its millions of white lights like silver leaves, always passing, never gone, says such inimitably witty things that even the thin, old-maidish reeds are bent double with laughter, though they whisper, 'Hush, hush, hush!' for propriety's sake. There the termagant wind comes hurtling, roaring with rough, good-humoured merriment, when the long-tailed tits, with all their dignity gone and their tails blown over their heads, look like balls of wool with a knitting-needle stuck in at an acute angle. There in June the cuckoo-pint plays a game of her own invention with the inquiring, greedy little flies who come to see her because she keeps a good table. She lets them all in, opening the door and disclosing a dainty repast. When they are inside, clap goes the door, a shower of pollen falls over back and wings, and there they have to stay at her pleasure; but she lets them go in an hour or two.

In spring, if you brush a branch aside, you find it weighted with a burden of life. At some junction of the branches nestles the round home, full to overflowing of panting, vociferous, helpless youth. The warm little bodies, the eager beaks, opening with one impulse in the enthusiastic hope that food is coming, the crude, yet sweet young voices – the delicious surprise of these never grows dull.

The path is full of white butterflies, that have risen from flowery fields beyond the sea, lighting with a flicker of wings on the rigging of some yacht, and so coming across at their ease. There the queen bee with her strange, low piping – a mere breath of sound, but stirring the same frenzy as bagpipes played softly before a battle – wakens madness in her followers, and lures them through the gates of adventure as Ned Puw's fiddle inveigled folk through the gates of Faery. There, in winter, you can find little caterpillars huddled together in a silk marquee, at which they have all toiled like good communists. In summer, the Pedlar's-basket – a saxifrage – shows her gay wares and ribands of red stalk; the mulleins – the hig-tapers of the Saxons – burn, pale yellow, on each side of the path, but when the moon goes behind a cloud, they suddenly extinguish their torches, leaving us to play catch-as-catch-can with the teazels in the dark.

When the enchanter's nightshade shone palely along the way, and the moonlight barred it with black and silver, I went tiptoe upon the seeding moss to look for little owls. Over the path stretched a polished beech bough; behind it, like an enormous lemon, hung the moon; upon it, still and silent and inimitably grave, were two baby owls taking an airing. They stared at me, not because I was interesting – they made me feel that – but because I was there. The four eyes were focused like cameras in a certain direction, and anything that came within the line of vision was necessarily taken in by them. One waited with the concentrated longing of the photographed for the little click of release. It never came, and I realized that this was to be an endless exposure. Their double stare awed me like the gaze of a thought-reader. It was perfectly useless to stare back, because it was obvious that they could go on like that interminably. I walked round the tree; but as I went, the two heads came round also with one effortless movement, and without the visible ruffling of a single fluffy feather. Over their backs the four eyes continued to gaze at me uncannily. They were even more impressive now, because they were facing the moon. So philosophical and so old they seemed, that one could not imagine them in the undignified confinement of mere eggs; yet in that ridiculous position they had been only a short time ago. Simon Stylites could not have ignored earth and gazed into space with more abstraction than they. A long, weird cry came creeping through the wood. Soon the soft, swooping wings of the mother owl would bring her down the moonlight. At the cry I was sure that a slightly interested look dawned in the four eyes; it passed instantaneously, and the stare was cold on me again. Then they began to snore. This was too much. Knowing their pertinacity, I was sure that they would not stop until they were fed. 'Good night, Methuselahs!' I said, dropping them a curtsey, and ran down the glade, silently laughing and questioning of the look of interest. Ever since, the remembrance of those aloof babies has been a wizard's wand to conjure laughter. In just the same solemn way young swallows stare at you over the side of their nest, when they have reached the boiling-over stage and can see the world. Perhaps the solemnity is a disguise. Wagtails are easier to understand, their comedy being cruder. They rush furiously over soft mud; apparently no one wins the race, but all return with the air of victors, jerking their tails. Swifts are not subtle either; they wheel and scream until they become hysterical and forget all decorum in their mad games – Olympia caricatured in the stadium of the air.

If we love the creatures of earth, who are so gaily irresponsible, so full of zest, we shall share with them the large-hearted merriment of comradeship, and find that the blessing of the helpless is the key to unlock the world. In laughing whole-heartedly a man must attain a certain freedom from selfishness, a certain purity; and the greatest saints are the merriest-hearted people. Down that path of rosy mint and astringent fennel the laughter is like Gerard's sanicle – 'a thing to make whole and sound all inward hurts and outward wounds.' For love is health to the innermost being, and every time we laugh there, love deepens.

Lately I went where the track leads across stepping-stones to the gleaming water meadows. Lady's-smocks were nodding down the way, shining faintly, spiritlike and gay in their lingering euthanasia. Great moths flapped up in the silver dew, streaked and dappled with ash-grey and cadmium, and small ones came by continually, palpitating down the dusk: but by an alder was one that neither flapped nor flew. He simply held his wings straight out and rotated on his own axis, as a Dervish dances. As he ascended mysteriously in the dark, he seemed to be whimsically pointing out to the others, who flew so madly from field to copse and back again, that for all the good they did, they might just as well spin in one place. He was the ghost-swift, and he turned stilly, with ethereal grace, above one spot because, somewhere in the dark grass, on a wet blade, hung his mate, unseen except by him. To her, warm-golden in the chilly evening, he would speed like a falling star, when he had won her by his grace and his glimmering armour.

After awhile I came to a great gnarled hawthorn hedge, cloudy with blossom and tinged with pink – for flowering time was nearly over. Within its precincts dwelt intense sweetness; and there I stayed, looking into the next field through an interstice of the twisty branches. The young rabbits were out under the moon, wild with excitement, the very soul of gaiety: they were washing their faces, dashing off at a tangent, leaping over lakes of pale light. Parents, grandparents, and great-grandparents were there, frisking with abandon in the athletic manner of Dickens's old folk at Christmas. Off went a stripling, bounding over a lake, landing in the middle, dashing away with a delighted kick, as if he said – 'Ha! Only moonshine water!' A grandfather, watching as he trimmed his whiskers, was fired to do likewise, gleefully beating the record. What is that stir in the grass at the root of the thorn? A grave hedgehog slips out and watches in a superior manner. Suddenly she becomes infected with the revelry, and rushes away at a surprising pace to share the general energy of enjoyment. Behind her come four minute hedgehogs, replicas of their mother, except that their spines are nearly white and their ears hang down. Like her, they run in the manner of toy animals upon invisible wheels. They all go at a speed one could not have believed possible, joining in the fun, recklessly negotiating the fairy rings; and their absurd little shadows follow madly after.

Let us go hunting marvels down this gay path, where larch and hazel hang out their rosy flowers; where green curtains of mist hide more miracles; where there are wet forget-me-nots beside the grey cloud-lakes; where rainbows are; where the aspens lean against the warm west and seem to murmur of a Being in whose presence we may rejoice unafraid.

We are so overwhelmed, in these days, with our discoveries of omnipotence that we have little time for realizing the minute care allied with it. We forget that the power which sets the parhelion flaming in the sunset, and calls the straying comet back from the bounds of the dark, also puts the orange underwing to sleep in her chrysalis cradle, while the flower she loves best is prepared for her. Who can say which is the greater sign of creative power, the sun with its planet system swinging with governed impetus to some incalculable end, or the gold sallow catkin with its flashing system of little flies? Ephemera, all of them; and all utterly beyond our understanding.

We see nature 'red in tooth and claw,' and so it is;

181

but it is so much else as well; it is dewy, it is honey-sweet, it is full of the soft voices of young creatures and the reassuring tones of motherhood. Year by year innumerable acorns under the soil take off their fustian coats and begin their long climb. Year by year, out of the mud that seems so ugly, up the green rushes comes the delicate dragon-fly, and sets the air on fire.

Beauty

The Beauty of Form

'Who was he whose pencil drew the whole round of the sun?'

VIRGIL

MAN can never hope to touch, in things of his making, the perfection of the forms of nature. His most magnificent architecture is dwarfed by the structure of natural things. The purest classic curve – so satisfying because so gentle, so quickening to the imagination because it leads the mind on to wish for the completion of the circle – seems small beside the curve of the horizon. The height and poetry of clustered columns dwindle beside the thousand pillars of the forest. It is not only the immensity of nature that makes the difference; it is something deeper; it is the contrast between creative genius and mere constructive art. Man makes things piece by piece, shaping them from outside, but natural forms come from within; there is no mosaic work; the creation grows up perfect in itself. These things live; though we call trees inanimate, it is really only man's structures that are so; no living germ is in his pillar, as in the heart of an oak. Only in the intangible things of the mind can man approach this creative power, and even then it is seldom that a thought springs up in faultless symmetry into music or poetry. The grass-blade rising from its sheath in unassuming perfection is more marvellous in its immanent beauty than the two-edged blade of a legendary angel sword. Where did the first shaping happen? Was the blade there when the sheath began to push through the soil, or when it

185

lay ready to emerge in minute integrity from the root? The same curiosity is awakened by the small brown bud at the end of a chestnut twig in autumn, a little further on than this year's fruit. How much of the future form is hidden in that small sphere? How much embryo tree is wrapped in its inner cases of wool and velvet? What hint of next summer's white chalice and green finger dwells in its innermost recesses? Long before the unfolding of these buds in April, when the downy leaflets uncurl, you can see, if you open one, the compressed cluster – each yellowish ball about the size of a pinhead – which is the future flower, and the faint dawnings of leaves all wrapped in soft wadding. The thought of the sap forming itself into these marvels, of the skilful silent artistry going on without hands at the end of every bough and at the heart of every root makes the world a place of almost unbearable wonder.

The absolute silence makes this more impressive after one has realized it, but sometimes it makes one forget what is happening. Man's work is accompanied by so much noise; if he desires a silver cup for sacraments, there must go to its fashioning the sound of hammering, the scratch of a chisel, the roar of a furnace; but when the innumerable chalices of the privet are made ready for the hawk-moth's first taste of honey there is no stir at all. The aisles and transepts of our temples rise with clamour of voices and commotion of labour; even the poetic silence of Solomon's building meant tumult somewhere; but the aisle of pines down a mountain side, the transept of beeches in a valley, rise as softly as a thought into majestic completeness. A crocus achieves her end; her curving cup stands up in the light and air in spite of the weight of inanimate matter pressing on her from all sides during her upward progress; with thin petals folded close in the delicate pointed case, she comes through scathless and silent.

Not only does this formative power triumph over all obstacles in producing its special symmetry, but it evolves countless variations of it from one germ of life – as in the pear-tree's lattice-work of little twigs, pillars of trunk and branch, flat oval leaves, round five-petalled flowers, pitcher-shaped calix, pointed seeds and fruit like a falling raindrop.

Stranger than this complexity is the continuity of individual forms. What slumbers in the fourfold seed-case of the beech, and is essentially different in result from the embryo in the winged samara of an elm? The beech leaves that Virgil loved before Christianity came into the world throw the same shadows on our churches as they did on the forest altars of Pan. Every year the daisy root sends up its little rayed disk.

When, long ago, Odoric of Pordenone left the snowy Alps for the Himalayas, snow crystals of the same forms still fell round him. These complex and lovely figures, condensing upon their mysterious nucleus of cosmic dust, always keep the same intrinsic structure. Feathered stars, roses set in ferns, rayed trefoils, sea-weed-like fronds full of little suns, they have all the same angles and are made hexagonally.

Just as a certain air, introduced continually in a piece of music, expresses the idea of the composer, so this perpetual reincarnation of the same cabalistic signs in nature might help us, if we could gather the scattered meanings, to a clearer understanding of the plasmic force behind them – a force patient and vast, vouchsafing no explanation. In this occult script the world might find a new bible of spiritual enlightenment – a writing, not in fire upon tables of stone, but in subtile traceries on young leaves and buds. Have not all symbolic artists, children, and priests of new religions some intuition of this? For the thought – so dim and so dear – that all fine contours are a direct message from God, is rooted deep in the minds of the simple-hearted, who are the Magi of the world.

We see, now that Christianity has interpreted it for us, the significance of the cross – that monogram of Christ and *cote-armure* of pity, built up somewhere in the branches of almost every tree, stamped in the centre of almost every flower. Humanity had learnt to make the cross long before that mild night when the flocks cried across the slopes of Bethlehem and their keepers whispered of visions. It may be that if Christ had not died, the meaning of the cross would have been revealed in some other way.

The circle, with its segments – curve, crescent semicircle – is another letter of the multitudinous alphabet. One of the loveliest variations of it is the chalice, where the centre has receded so that the flower is at once round and deep. In all cup-shapes and trumpet-shapes there is the fascination of this remote centre where the heart of the bloom dwells. Two of the most beautiful of these are the white convolvulus, Sar

Graal of the hedges, and the dwale – that lurid amphora where the death's-head moth, with its weird form and wings of enchanted purples, drinks under the white light of the moon and, if it is touched, cries out like a witch in a weak, strident voice.

The world is based on curves; for each of us morning means the growing circle of the sun; we wait in storms for the grand half-circle of the rainbow, which is far more impressive in its governed sweep – embracing the world – than in the flaming of its seven-divided colours. There is nothing so restful as a perfect circle, whether seen, as in the full moon, or implied, as in the young crescent. It is a symbol of things men feel but cannot understand; so Merlin 'made the round table in token-ing of the roundness of the world'; so Vaughan saw eternity 'like a great Ring.' Nearly all essential things are round – the perianth of flowers, where the seed is, stars, the window of the eye. Lines, after all, are only for measuring circles; the diameter of the earth is un-important in itself. Though perspective has an extra-ordinary power of bringing wonder – hunger for the far away, fear of the future – it must be a long per-spective; a piece of road or a tree must attain a certain length or height before it haunts the imagination. But a circle, however small, is immutable, holds infinity; because of this, and because of the implied centre, it is the most perfect symbol of Divinity.

All green things that have to cleave their way come into the light like swords – grass, leaves emerging from the sheath, shoots splitting the bark – all these are pointed. In the outermost branch and the topmost twig of a tree the point sharply defines the limit of the individual form as it stands against the vagueness of air. The point is where thought slips from the finite to the infinite, like a bird balanced on the top of a fir-tree before he trusts himself to immensity. 'At the point of death' has in it something of this idea of the sudden ending of a form, where the topmost shoot of mortality ceases upon the eternal. The circle is static, the point dynamic.

Man finds in the plastic beauty of earth revelations for his practical needs. It is as if the forms of nature waited through the centuries until the moment comes for man to gather the ripe idea in them. The acanthus gave its curve to Greek sculpture. The symmetry of many plants is akin to the spirit of ancient peoples – woad, with leaves like roughly made arrow-heads; golden saxifrage, with its calix like a Roman urn; meadow-vetchling, with its curious stipules like spear-heads locked in conflict. Wandering once in June over some Roman ruins in an English field, I was struck by the strange kinship between the plants that now carpet the place and the men who once lived there. Perhaps some Roman, gathering saxifrage for medicine, wondered at the perfection of the little cup, and designed one like it. Or an armourer, looking idly at the lathyrus stipules, may have gained from them the idea for a new kind of spear. Earlier still, a British boy plucking woad may have chipped an arrow-head in imitation of it. In the hot silence of the broken walls the saxifrage cup was as redolent of Rome as the glass urn that was found buried there; the lathyrus leaves, like spears and swords mong the scarlet banners of the poppies, recalled the glory of cohort and legion.

To know the beauty of earth's lineaments, one must watch them through the seasons. Spring is the time of points and immature half-rounds, when everything is folded. There is a gradual thickening of outline, a massing of shapes, a growing indefiniteness of branch and twig. The intrinsic structure of winter is being veiled by the new, extrinsic forms. Leaves cover the bare hawthorn; flowers foam over the leaves. Then comes summer; the underlying frame is obliterated. When the woods are flooded with bloom, the leaves are almost unnoticed; when the country is aswing with music and alight with colour and the fields are full of seeded grass, the curves of the flower are softly effaced and rounded into the regnant fruit. Then autumn sends a wind in the treetops; twig after twig emerges from the ramifications of foliage; the little birch discards her last raiment, and stands erect in essential beauty with every graceful branch delicately outlined on the sky; the ash looks as fine as maidenhair with its intricate traceries interspersed with brown samaras. The most ethereal forms belong to winter; hers is the beauty that the leaf has when substance and sap are gone and only the frail white outline remains. This is the best time to learn the proportions of things. The lack of this period of stern outline must make a difference in the character of the inhabitants of lands that never know any cessation of luxuriance. In a winter landscape – especially in a wood – there is the same kind of purity that the Greeks saw in the unclad human form; it is like a young athlete, ready for racing with his flowing garments flung aside. It is an education in restraint; after seeing it, one cannot forget the fine severity beneath all natural beauty.

There is no impressionism in a tree or a hill; under the irregularities of colour, the splashes and brilliant gleams, is the line-perfection in which the impressionism of art fails. An artist can transfer the acacia to canvas in a series of green and white dots and blurs, but he does not achieve all the beauty, for beneath the tree's arborescence is the fineness of an etching. The knowledge that under the chestnut's thick curtains and the aspen's tremulous foliage is a faultless frame gives the trees an honour beyond mere surface beauty. It is this austerity in even the airiest thing, like a butterfly's wing, that makes the study of form ennobling. We do not know why the springing straightness of a bough, the cup-like hollow in an apple petal, the gentle curves that meet at the end of a laburnum leaf, are so lovely; we only feel their delight. It may be because in all these shapes there is nothing extraneous, nothing unfinished. The flower has no unnecessary petal; the birds' homes are wholly complete.

We can gain a grasp of this wonder of structure from a seed of groundsel or a sparrow's feather picked up in the street; for a spray of plumy meadowsweet or one dandelion floret is a poem in itself, and the sand particle is complex, curiously fashioned and polished. The triangles, ovals, trefoils and eared circles of pollen are minutely perfect. The pollen grain of chicory – an outer and inner haxagon united by rays – is a rose window in a shrine of lapis lazuli. It needs no light behind it, for it illumines itself. Within is no mere painting, but a powerful principle, an active creature, the architect of next year's sky-blue temple. There is a striking unity in some flowers between the shape of the pollen grain and that of the calix and corolla. The open chicory flower and the pollen grain are both polygonal and rayed from the centre. The pollen grain of the passion flower – like a round filagree box with a lid – is almost exactly the same in construction as the centre of the flower with its enamelled cut-work of stamen, stigma and filament.

Apart from colour, form is awe-inspiring because it seems to be the outcome of mind alone. The marble whiteness and stillness of a statue, and the greatest of Greek tragedies – these strike coldly on the heart; for their creators were occupied with form and intellect to the exclusion of more emotional things. A skeleton is terrifying for the same reason. At the thought of the mountains in the moon, and of all places of a kindred desolation upon earth, we tremble; in these majestic and gloomy formations no stir or gleam hides from us the fearful vision of what the world might have been if its economy had not included the kindly and comforting developments of life – motion and colour.

The forms of nature seem to speak of the ageless and omnipotent life of their Cause, who formed the round reed in the marsh for the music of Pan, the rugged upland tree for the cross of Christ. Man's ingenuity cut and notched the reed for joy and bound the wood straitly for pain; but the hollow reed and the ash tree were not of his shaping any more than the wild melody of the syrinx or the magnificent silence of Calvary were of human impulse.

The Beauty of Shadow

'They seated themselves under the shade of this white
thorn, and took their solace.'

OLD ROMANCE

SHADOW is one of the easiest to perceive of all
nature's beauties. As one may see the charm of a pro-
file for the first time when looking at a silhouette, so one
becomes aware of the perfection of a natural outline more
quickly by seeing it drawn in one colour. It is much sim-
pler to trace the fairy fretwork of a mountain ash when
it lies on the grass in shadow than when the eyes are
dazzled by the vivid green and clustering scarlet of berry
and leaf against the sky. It has become a blue tree
on the green canvas of a field. Without shadow things
would seem unreal, unbreathing as figures in a dream –
flat, unrelieved tapestry on the walls of the world. With
it come reality and rounded loveliness. It is only the
bare winter tree, the barren heart, that are shadowless.

The colours of shadows vary with climate and season;
they are mauve on ripe corn, deeply black on hot, white
roads in summer, purple on ploughlands in sandstone
country, silver-grey on snow. Blue is their prevailing
colour, varying from the sapphire of Love-in-a-Mist to
the indigo at the root of a thundercloud.

In motion as well as in tint these astral bodies of
material things have an ever-changing individuality –
faithfully following or waiting beside their prototypes.
They flit with the birds, small winged spirits, and even
a bee's wing, so unsubstantial itself, has a faint replica
that follows its airy fanning. The shade of a leaf

caresses its own flower and its fellow-leaf with gentle strokings; and when a cherry blossom falls down the chequered steeps of the tree, a little mournful shadow goes with her. The shade of the tendrilled creeper steals into a room and lies along the floor, an emissary from the plant outside that peers in but cannot enter. The somnolent gloom thrown by the massed foliage gives majesty to the summer field; and how splendid on some loud day in the equinox, is the sight of the dumb shadows of the shouting, gesticulating trees tossing and bending, lengthening and shrinking over the land. Cloud-shadows on a plain are inexpressibly alluring. Some are like a mere breath on a mirror, others are dark and ominous, passing into the distance only to be replaced by fresh phalanxes, as though some conquering army had gone forth. But they are most stately over mountains, for they alone have power to darken the everlasting summits.

Midday, the period of practicality, is fitly unshadowed; perhaps that is why it has so little glamour. But when the tired labourer turns homeward in the evening, he is led or followed by a lengthening shade; every tree and hedge sends forth a little mimic to join the ranks; the sheep and cattle walk the fields with shapes of primeval beasts behind them; houses stand half-circled in black moats; the world is barred with gold and purple. Now beside the runlets on the hill the pipkins of the mimulus, which have stood half full of shadow all day, brim over. Now the sharp, clear outline of the western hill steadily ascends its neighbour till all the heather has been quenched except the one ine of blood-red at the summit; the thick curtain covers that also, but it has no power over the immortal heavens. Then comes sleep, and deepens down the world. Out of shadow comes the dewy morning; into it retires the silent dusk. Out of it, one by one, we wander, our young eyes full of mystery; into it we all depart, when the noonday heat is past and the labourer turns home.

If you will go out on some June morning, before the earliest bee comes droning by, when the stripes of sunrise lie right across the awakening earth, you will know the fascination of shadows. On such a day they are almost as blue as chicory. As a child, I remember standing awe-stricken at the strange beauty of a well-known field in the magic of a June dawn. It had a line of tall trees in its eastern hedge, and if you watched while the sun rose, you saw what had been a wide, grey expanse suddenly spanned by swart, prostrate giants. It was as if, with one movement, every tree had flung itself upon its face – Mahommedan-wise – at the muezzin of sunrise. Perhaps the memory of such fresh delights, like dew in the flower-cup of life, may linger even after the flower is gathered. Quite early on a summer morning, if you look down an ugly street in a busy town, you will scarcely know it. The rows of houses have ceased to look dull, and have become the opposing camps of light and darkness; the street is a tessellated pavement of blue and yellow; the bush that looks so pathetically inadequate by day throws quite a forest of obscurity and becomes mysterious.

The shadow of a tree upon any house blesses it,

weaving with its cool, hypnotic gestures a soothin
quiet; but the place, of all human habitations, wher
it best loves to linger is a village street. There each lif
is framed in garden and orchard; companies of spirit
shapes go trembling up and down the humble walls an
roofs all day from the multitude of surrounding leave
in the highway the sunshine sleeps by the shadow of a
ivied wall – disturbed only once in an hour, and the
simply turning in its sleep. If those other shades, th
troubles of life, have become too dense and shoulderec
out the light, so that the sick imagination sees them a
crouching beasts of prey, a pilgrimage to such a trar
quil place in lilac time may help to set things right agai
In that sequestered road, where the whirr of a linnet
flight is startling, before the first workman come
through the dew, you can hardly fail to gather sor
share of peace. There, where the wet lilacs fling the
fragrance from garden to garden like bridges, and th
pale images of their massed blossom and heart-shape
leaves lie all along the way, questionings will seem
little unimportant – the shade-strewn road preaches
sweetly the necessity of interspersed dimness and ligh
By and by a door opens, and a labourer goes whistlir
down the chequered track that is so like his life. Her
even death loses some of its grimness – its hideousne
of association, which is so unnecessary. For the ima;
ination sees the highway of mortal existence where
ends abruptly, penumbrous, flecked with shade fro:
the heart-shaped leaves of the Tree of Life: and tl
shadow is the sign that we have come at last within tl
pale of the tree's mysterious whisperings.

The slightly blurred colours of reflections – water-
shadows – are more vivid than reality, as if water were
a brighter medium than air; what they lose in strength
of outline through the motion of the current, they gain
in dreamy charm. Were ever forget-me-nots half so
blue as those that gaze skyward from clear water? Did
you know all the sweetness of flushed wild-rose faces
until you saw them sleeping in a stream? Some spell
lies on rivers where willows bend over them and trans-
fuse them with tender green, with depths of swaying
leaf-reflections, lighter in the centre, where the over-
hanging tracery shows the sky, very dark at the sides,
where the grassy banks are steep and the leaves thick.
Such beauty brings the longing (almost a torment to
some minds) to be absorbed in nature, dissolved in it
even to the losing of personality. Perhaps the person
who most nearly approaches this oneness physically is
a boy who plunges into a green pool in the early morning. Spiritually, the Greeks came near it, with their
legends of maidens melting into laurels or becoming
nightingales after death. Beside a full-flowing river in
autumn this longing is strong and urgent. Coming
round a curve, you stop with a sudden intake of the
breath, dazzled by a blaze of glory. There stands on
the bank and there lies in the flood a tree of beaten gold,
gently moving against the sky, gently quivering in the
water, flinging largess of its yellow money into the
instaed gold of its reflection. The sun makes each leaf
transparent, and the whole picture is ardent as the face
of some angel of a flaming star. As the spirit strives to
gather some of the beauty, it longs to be less finite, less

bounded; it desires an infinite future in which to reflect universal loveliness.

When the sun and the wind are abroad together watch the cloud-reflections hurrying along with the current of a river, or travelling up-stream. This last is like the striving of two wills for the mastery; the froth of the current and the foam of the clouds continually cross.

In glassy lakes the surrounding woods meet in the depths of the water, and make a strange, new world No wonder there are so many legends of villages and churches under meres, and bells ringing eerily below the water-lilies. Looking down into the limpid quiet where everything is so familiar, yet so alien, the eye sees, beyond those mysterious green glades, habitation of the water-country, twisted of chimney as an elfin chateau, blurred replicas of some cottage on the bank wavering in outline and impossible in perspective Almost one can see the inhabitants passing at the end of the glades, or a white hand waving from the window of an unsubstantial dwelling. Almost one can see the gleaming arm of some water-maiden – Aigle or Vivian of the Lake – beckoning, bare and beautiful, or clad in shining samite. Though there is no Hylas now to be charmed into the green silence, no Excalibur to be lifted above the mere, yet there is still magic in these reflections.

On calm, hot days, water sends up over bank and tree vacillating, shimmering patterns that waver to the tree top and back again, like flocks of hovering golden birds Far within clear water dwells the sun's twin brother there the pale sister of the moon goes sailing; there the stars glimmer, spreading into little moons, shrinking into mere points of light at the will of the water.

When we look down into the blueness of some little pool, rejoicing in the birdlike passage of the clouds, and then look up to the wide sky, we realize that the finite is like a lake which, as far as its capacity allows, mirrors the infinite; and when we see the foreshortened image of a poplar stretched in pale colouring beneath it, we have a sudden vision of time as the faint, straitened shadow of eternity.

The Beauty of Colour

'The Sunne shone
Upon my bed with bright bemes,
With many glad gilden stremes,
And eke the welkin was so faire,
Blew, bright, clere was the air.'

CHAUCER

A ROSE that flushes in the bud grows pure white in maturity; a sycamore leaf, from the moment of its soft uncurling, changes a little day by day until the final flame of the year; so the colours of all things fluctuate continually. They seem to float round material forms, migratory, never a changeless possession of any. Nightly the darkness washes them out with her dusky brush, and in the strong hands of the seasons they are ephemeral. When the hazy freshness thickens daily round an alder-trunk, one can hardly believe that anything so ethereal emanates from the black bark; it is like a green gossamer from the evening west caught in the branches. Blossoming time in a damson country, when the whiteness foams over valley and ridge, has the same effect of clouds resting on the trees. To the eye of imagination all things stand haloed in colour that flickers and quickens mysteriously.

However much we may learn of chlorophyl, chromogen, and colour-cells – the pigments of nature that are made from earth and rain, air and sun, somewhere in the dark habitation of the roots and the airy galleries of the leaves – we do not know why the same ingredients should clothe one petal with flame and another with blue. We do not know what impulse sends up the water-lily from the stagnant ooze in glistening white, and lays a mauve mantle over the wistaria that feeds upon corruption; nor why two plants of the same genus in the same conditions should be so differently coloured as are the blue and yellow gentian. Colour like fragrance, is intimately connected with light; and between the different rays of the spectrum and the colour-cells of plants there is a strange telepathy. These processes, so little explored, seem in their deep secrecy and earthly spirituality more marvellous than the most radiant visions of the mystics.

Of all colours, brown is the most satisfying. It is the deep, fertile tint of the earth itself; it lies hidden beneath every field and garden; it is the garment of multitudes of earth's children, from the mouse to the eagle; the men of the fields are russet-clad and russet-complexioned; thousands of seeds, from the heavy burr to the breeze-blown thistle-fluff, are brown as the soil from which they come, to which they return; and of the same fruitful colour are the rushing streams, the pillars of the forest, and the buttresses of the hills. It is dim with antiquity, full of the magic that lurks within reality; and just as one stands in an ancient hall, gazing into the duskiness and waiting for the coming of departed inhabitants, so one watches and listens in the tawny furrowlands for the tread of the myriads whose lives have gone to the making of them. There is that in brown which surely speaks to all who are ever born into the world.

Green is the fresh emblem of well-founded hopes. In blue the spirit can wander, but in green it can rest.

A picture of vivid contrasts could be painted in green alone; there are a hundred shades of it in one field – malachite, beryl, emerald, and all the intermediate tints. Uncurling oak-leaves have a dash of blue and a great deal of sienna; daffodil leaves and holly are blue-green: young larches are sky and gamboge; there is a great deal of red in the tender young leaves of birches; fir-needles have a whitish line on the underside; yews are black-green; the laburnum is toned with grey. Because it is so plentifully mixed with other colours, it is never crude. It also has endless variations of transparency and opacity; beech leaves in May are so pellucid that you can almost see through them; rhododendrons are so solidly coloured that they reflect the light. The best of all greens are in the tender plants of spring woods and meadows – the anemone, the red-spotted sorrel, ferns of fine texture, glaucous mosses, sedges even cooler to look upon than water. Not a place on earth need be destitute of green; the desert has its cactus, the sea its translucent weed. However poor a man may be, he can have a sprig of green by his door, even if it is only a trail of ivy in a broken jar. The saddest place can have its green shoot of hope, the same hope that irradiates the burgeoning forest. Deep in men's hearts there lives this spirit of hope – or religion – renewed each spring. Over churches of the sternest creeds the ivy is not afraid to climb; and when the church has crumbled with its dogma, the ivy covers all with its kindly curtain and speaks of a life greater than these, and an evergreen love that embraces all.

Those hot splendours of sunrise and sunset, of first

and last things – red and gold – are the colours of all man loves – wealth and the blood that is poured to gain it, scarlet lips and yellow hair, the sacramental chalice and the wine within. Nature is prodigal of them, and autumn is their festival, with its shining pavements of harvest, its sierras of flaming bracken, its burning woods and smouldering hedges and trees like tongues of orange and red flame. No coolness of the blue above, no liquidness of silver nights can quench their fierceness until they have consumed their prey. They are the colours of crises; in stormy dawns they put the darkness to flight with their bright scimitars, and stain the streams and possess the sky. To them belongs ripeness – apple and pomegranate and the tree of the knowledge of good and evil. To them belong the haughty beauty of tropical flowers and the terrible loveliness of fire, and a blood-red blossom with a golden heart is the ancient emblem of passion.

Mauve has a delicate artificiality, something neither of earth nor heaven. It is like the temperament which can express in sheer artistic pleasure heights and depths which it can never touch. Whether it is sultry, as in lilac, or cool, as in lady's-smocks, this mingling of fierce red and saintly blue has an elfin quality. Hence comes the eeriness of a field of autumn crocuses at twilight, when every folded flower is growing invisible, and doubtless there is a fairy curled up in each. Children look for the Little People in mauve flowers – Canterbury bells and hyacinths – and, though they never find them, they know them there. Mauve enchants the mind, lures it to open its amethyst door, and behold!

nothing but emptiness and eldritch moonshine. It is a Vivian crowned with nightshade and helleborine, leading with soft allurements to a country whose shores are of vanishing mist.

Silver is akin to mauve. Foam and icicles, dandelion clocks in the sun, the moon and stars, white flowers under the moon – all have this pristine tint that is more a radiance than a colour, that is without depth or shadow, with a fleetingness like that of dreams. It is the colour of the undersides of things. White-willow and poplar leaves are lined with it; watching them, one is reminded of the moment when a friend unexpectedly turns his remoter self towards one – his white self that is so easily transfigured. When the wind is in a plane-tree, the multitudes of leaves are suddenly ruffled, so that the whole tree shines; it is like watching a crowd of people under some soul-stirring emotion. Half the charm of silver in nature is due to its remoteness; no ore of man's refining can attain the sparkle of a rain-drop; we cannot distil the radiance from a white narcissus, nor rob the stars of their silver fleeces. There is a perfect harmony of mauve and silver in a birch wood a little while before the leaves come. The shining stems rise out of a faint purple mist which deepens in the distance. Above, all the twigs are softly purple too, and, being very fine and numerous, they make another haze higher up. The straight silver rods gleam in long perspective in their setting of cloudy violet, lost in it above and below. Any face might look out from that mist, any white feet of nymph or hamadryad pass among the glimmering aisles; in the dim, lilac-tinted distance it may be that Merlin still sleeps in his vaporous magic circle.

Blue is the rarest colour, the one which least often imprisons itself in material things. There are few blue flowers, and most of them are small and fragile, like love-in-a-mist and speedwell. Gentian is never so lavishly outspread as it is upon the heights, symbolically near the sky. Blue expanses – reflections in water, the cobalt of distance, are only lent to earth. If we want endless, satisfying blue, we must look up to where it dwells in impalpable space, shining like solid enamel, or liquid and vague. There is the roaming-place of the mystic; through the dissolving azure of a summer day he tries to probe; into the impenetrable heavens of night he launches his spirit like a coracle among the stars. Blue is a holy colour; the Sufis wore it with this significance, and it is fitly used for Madonnas' robes and temple hangings, since the temple of our conscious and unconscious worship is canopied with it. Often a flash of sapphire in water, a shade of turquoise in the sky, will strike across the heart with an inexplicable pang. It is not sorrow; it is more than joy; it is at once the realization of a perfect thing, the fear that we may never see it again, and the instinct that urges us to ascend through the known beauty to the unknown which is both the veil and the voice that summons beyond it.

Though winter may wear a sad-coloured garment, it is shot with bright threads of reminiscence and prophecy. Orange oak leaves, lingering seed-vessels on ash and lime, crimson blackberry trails, are recollections of past splendour. The sere and broken reeds and rushes – golden and russet – are like the piled trophies of some fairy warfare; spear and sword and bulrush-banner recall the time when conquering summer led forth his legions. There are dreams and dawnings of another summer also. The twigs that look so lifeless have minute buds on them, vivid points of colour. The alder's purple buds and dripping gold of catkins, the red knobs on larches, the sticky, brown chestnut-buds, the green buds of the sycamore, are all brilliant and warm with sleeping summer. The purple osier is already set with green points from which are to emerge fluffy catkins, and the sallow is preparing its gold and silver blossoms which are to be the early palm, dripping with honey and humming with insects. There are pale blooms of box and ivy; fir-cones rich as pine-apples in the sun, with flashes of blue-tits' wings about them; red pine trunks; shining greys of ash and beech bole; vivid green of elder-trees; holly (Robin Hood of the woods) flames in red and green; blue-grey birds scud across the dim, tufted meadows. The distant woods grow auburn as the leaf-buds swell, and in their folds the shadows are like dwale. After the turn of the year the tops of the poplars and aspens take the colour of ripe oats. Wild-fire runs along the elms as the red buds push out. In February is the bridal of the yew, when one tree is covered with small wax cups – the future berries – and another is thick with honey-coloured flowers; then, at the least breeze, the air is full of the gold dust of pollen. In dark November comes the heyday of the mother-tree. She flushes into young rose, tender as pink hawthorn, but deeper; all her sombre recesses of ancient green are transfigured by this surprise of beauty, by these multitudes of japonica-tinted berries. At each spray's end flutter missel-thrushes, their spread wings lined with silver. Upon the dark-green background this harmony of rose and pearl glows like an old illumination; its unobtrusiveness deepens the charm. Only the undersides of the branches glimmer with colour, only the underwings have a moon-lit look; yet it is enough, since we know that the dark wings can be transfigured, that the melancholy trees can sometimes stand beneath the pale sky in a rosy haze, as if ethereal dew had distilled upon them. The spirit of the picture is reminiscent of Orcagna's *Assumption of the Virgin* in alabaster, where angels hover round a berry-shaped mandorla in which Mary is throned.

Atmosphere, that whimsical artist, transforms the already brilliant world by clothing things in tints other than their own. A wide sweep of country fascinates us not only by its innate beauty but by the airy blue of the far plain, the smoking woods, the hills like wet violets. The haze that clings in the hearts of autumn trees, that foams like a white sea round the stems in a larch copse, and hangs – pale lavender – in the recesses of beech woods, lends the trees more loveliness than their own. Brimming the valleys, dimpling the fields, it is the magic of a March morning; looming over hills, it adds mystery to their strength of outline. Near sunset, soft films gather imperceptibly, stealing over everything, so that all colours, while keeping their individuality, are mixed with gold medium. The clearest atmosphere throws a veil over actual things; upon even a near horizon trees seldom look green, but are etched upon the clouds in pale peacock and silver-grey, flaming at the sun's pleasure into bronze and copper. Often the most ordinary scenery puts on such colours as no painter would dare to imitate; whoever cares to look may see his neighbour's barn standing in the celestial radiance of *Revelations* or the fantastic brilliance of elfdom. They can see ploughland red in the sunset, as though stained with the blood of generations; topaz pastures; hedges of the blue of Gobelin tapestry; valleys sheeted in silver, when the rising mist and the descending moonlight are interfused. In heavy, thunderous weather the earth returns to the iron age; everything is sombre, hard and grey until the sky grows hot for the melting and gives things the metallic look of lustre-ware. Sometimes in snow a miracle of air and light transforms the world into a great glowing rose. Atmosphere has no abiding place, no set rules for its coming and going; when you walk upon the hills, their watchet raiment fades, and you cannot carry home the primrose mist of morning. All the more appealing is this vagrant glamour, because it only brushes the solid earth with swallow wings.

The best way of seeing colour unallied with material form is to watch the sky; and when everything else is gone, it shines on still above us. Once on a December evening the clouds were in three distinct layers of colour, each moving independently, blown by a different wind. First came ebony; beyond that, moving more slowly, a long, straight cloud of geranium; above that again, a soft stratum of brown; and through one tremendous gash in all three shone the kingfisher-blue sky. Low in the west, safe and far from the tempestuous masses, stood Hesperus; around him, ivory and crocus splashed the blue, and just above the distant hills lay a line of green.

On a November morning, when the sky was faint and clear, and a lake of light widened momentarily along the horizon, the moon stood high up with a star at her feet – pale silver. Another star, not so near, was soon merged in the oncoming tawny flood, which softly inundated every little crevice of the bare trees on the sky-line. Then in plunged the sun, swimming strongly, bent on reaching her, who thought herself so safe up there in the great expanses; and she paled and slid away with her attendant star, while he swam on with the tide of light that washed the sky.

Winter sunrise gives the impression that all colours have been drawn from the earth and set in the treasury of the heavens. There are the wild roses of summer hedges, the young green leaves of spring; there gold quickens, reminding us that the sun has not forgotten his daffodils; and the world warms her frozen breast in the reflected glory. Often in the life of the mind also the sky brightens as the earth fades. When the forlorn soul lies under a black frost and hears the long sigh of the snow-wind; when it seems that no shoot of hope can ever rise from an existence so bound and burdened, reduced to almost imbecile passivity – then across the eternal heavens trail the essential colours of life, and the frozen spirit flushes into rose.

'You whom care in prison keeps,
And sickness doth suppress'

'You whom care in prison keeps, and sickness doth suppress'

'In his bed he may lie . . . and enjoy the whole world.'

SIR THOMAS BROWNE

ALONG these channels of Joy, Laughter, and Beauty vitality will flow into mind and body when other channels are dry and filled with drifts. Invalids are too much shut away from the golden unrest, the busy quiet of nature. When a doctor, who knows that earth is his ally, says – 'Take him out, distract his mind,' well-meaning relatives take him to the scenes of his past activity. They never find out their mistake because he tries with fierce determination 'not to be a fool'; he applauds with the rest when another man does what he once excelled in; but do we not all know that difficult smile of his? He is seeing, not the bright day and the blue eyes of hope, but the contrast between his former and his present self; to him the whole thing is a kind of horrible medicine; he prefers his sickroom. People without much imagination do not realize what pain they inflict when they persuade some girl who will never dance again 'just to come and watch.' They arrange everything for her physical comfort, and then show her – whose beauty is worn, whose girlish life is over – clearly and vividly what she has lost. Only a saint could bear this with equanimity. Not even a saint could benefit by it in bodily health. In nature there is a sure harbour; for things that once engrossed the mind begin to look pale and small when seen in conjunction with the immense, brilliant perspectives of hill and sky; so life's values right themselves again. The clean breath of truth blows through this tameless world; here are no enervating doctrines of the need of punishment through sickness; here is no unwholesome atmosphere of self-pity and apology for bodily disability.

It is hard, if people are young and eager for action, to be chained by physical weakness. It is grievous to be forced to lead a life of contemplation when the heart is set upon roaming – to be placed upon a philosophical hillside when you are all afire to be down in the plain amid the sweet, keen trouble of living. Yet a charm clothes all things seen from a hilltop. Nothing disturbs the quiet but such melodious sounds as the long iteration of a dove or the bleating of sheep – content hidden in melancholy. Through the still air come mysterious calls and echoes – remote as dreams, provocative to the imagination as a half-told romance. Looking into the world of nature from sickroom or garden, one finds out how lovely the near things are; the one tree or field will reveal depth on depth of beauty to the long, concentrated gaze.

When the sky after sunset is unclouded, except for some mauve lines in the east – like hyacinths under dew, sloping to a calm, blue sea – the cripple will wait with a deeper thrill than the rest of us for the coming of the moon. When she glides along the hyacinth banks – a silver boat, slipping into the sea, leaving in her wake a trail of foam – he can pass with her through the midnight skies as she moves, rudderless, with no mast, an argosy of dreams for men, threading the riding lights of the stars, sailing straight on to her harbour in the dawn, drawn up at last upon an opal shore.

The paralysed lad can send his heart with the gyr-falcon on a day's journey from blue-girdled Iceland to the Scottish homes of the rock-doves and back. Or he can go with the current of the great river that flows – like the rivers that watered Eden – with millions of side-channels and lesser streams but with ever undiminished velocity, from the uttermost point of the April tree-root to the uttermost point of the leaf, flowing faster than the blood in the body, and bearing on its flood the colour of the leaf, the scent of the flower.

Through any window may be seen the same gracious depths of blue air as Buddha contemplated through the interstices of his tree, as Michael Angelo saw through the windows of the Sistine chapel. The long gaze of a sick man may probe as far into the illimitable as they did. In the vast caverns of space, where Sirius lights the traveller, a genius and a weary invalid are equals – both frail as star-dust, both elder brothers of the sun. The reflections that will weave themselves across the beauty of earth, the sanity that a deep knowledge of earth gives, will help to a balanced judgment of the world's conflicts. Life in the green country makes philosophers, and humanity needs young philoso-phers, full of the intellectual fire and vigour that are lost in age. None are better fitted for this than they whose powers – circumscribed but unimpaired – are all focused on the mind, and who are honest thinkers because they live amid the integrity of nature.

For all who are cut off from complete spiritual inter-course with their fellows – who are in the world, but not quite of it – life is difficult and burdensome. But the loss of sight or hearing need not lessen their power of absorbing nature's messages and vitality; if they have lost the sunsets or the songs, these messages will be translated into a scent or a wave of sensation. One sense may bring dreams and echoes of another – you can see green water-shadows when the scent of meadowsweet is in the air, and hear remembered music when a certain light is on the hills. The satin touch of a peony petal recalls its pink sheen, and the feel of a silken barley sheath brings the surge and murmur of the field. The blind will hear the faintest notes in the music of earth, will feel touches soft as a moth's wing on hand and heart, will live in a world of elusive fragrances from which others are excluded. The deaf will see further into the rainbow than the rest of us; and the feel of water on the hand, air on the face, moss under foot, will be their service of song. Sweeter even than the exquisite things we know – transparencies, veins in leaves and flowers and in water where it bends over a fall, the cream and madder of pearbuds, the scent and music of rain – are the rare breaths and gleams that come only to a few. The blind and deaf can travel a long way, by the strength of their enforced concentration on the senses left to them, up the paths of light, scent and music, which seem to converge as they ascend, until they melt altogether in mystery. How far they will go and how much they will find out, no one can tell; but it is their benign work to show us the delicacy of creation – filling the spaces between the old, stable pleasures with these subtle new ones, like daffodils planted between apple trees.

These stricken men and women, from whom the world falls back as from a sanctuary where noise is muffled, may be aware, in the close and thrilling calm about them, of diviner existences, a more ethereal being. Then, gazing with the undimmed vision of the soul toward the ultimate Beauty, which is the meaning of all symbols, they will know the wonder that is a sacramental act of homage.

The men and women who most of all need peace are those who are smitten with some incurable disease. Their lives cannot be normal, and the sense of injustice and of difference from others, combined with their despair, saps what little strength they have. The seared spirit must have silence. In one of earth's tranquil haunts a man may lay his head on her green pillow. At first, perhaps, he will see death looming like a black chasm across his days. But when he has dwelt for a time between the green and the blue, when he has looked long at the broad skies and considered the punctual return of life after death in spring, it may be that he will come to the consciousness of Mystery brooding over the world; and because intuition tells him that death will take him a step nearer to this Mystery, he will cease to think of it as a chasm, and regard it rather as a gate on the skyline. Just as one stands at the foot of a steep field and sees in the hedge at the top a gate that opens on the blue, so he will see his short life as an upward slope – steep, but leading to a white gate swinging upon the infinite. He will have a heritage of joy while he climbs the ascent – sweet things about him, the warm comfort of some little creature's body pressed against face or heart, the pleasure of a bird's bright eyes looking into his, its fugitive wings pausing in their flight for him. He will know the wonder of a wild creature's confidence when, instead of eluding him, it seeks his friendship – a thing as strange and joyous as if a star came sweeping from her station to light upon his brow. The hearts of these dumb beings are sealed to us; their lives are wrapped in shadow. Might not the sick, by their genius for sympathy, help to bring the day when we shall cease to make ourselves ridiculous in the theatre of the cosmos by thinking that our neighbours, the people of the fields, were made for our sole benefit, and when corpses of the defenceless will be seen no more upon the tables of those who profess the gospel of love?

One who has lived under the large arbitrament of earth ceases to question. There is a hand on the hot forehead. He meets death with the absence of morbidity – almost amounting to indifference – which you find in the gay, short-lived citizens of wood and meadow. Death is no longer either the supreme disaster or the supreme desire, but an incident – the swinging back of the gate on the skyline. He begins to link himself with the Beauty that lies in and beyond the beauty of earth, like light in a flower; an intuition begins to dawn in him that this Beauty, or Love, is not only above all things, but in them, permeating them; that he and the very germ of disease that destroys his body abide in it as inevitably as the world abides in the invisible air. When each breath is drawn in this eternal atmosphere, now and forever are one; to-day and in a million years, here and beyond the uttermost star, we are in the heart of God.

In whatever way and to whatever extent people are set aside from the world, they can make their lives magnificent, bringing an evangel of peace to the travelworn companies of men. They dwell in the land of consolation, beside the healing watercourses – lilybordered, poplar-circled, flowing purely from the divine sea. In this land (no visible country) they are caught away into holiness by the vision that they see when a leaf unfolds, or when the birds make low, moonshiny music in the dusk. To them life comes pulsing down the sunbeam, whitening in the clover, fleeting in the wind.

If, invigorated by this vitality, cured of soul-sickness or body-sickness, they take up their work again, they may still live as the plant lives, whose every-day doings are a lyric. Walking among men with the light of their abiding joy in their eyes, they can beautify the workaday world; they can gather up Nature's ancient memories, her twining prophecies, and bind them about men's work and faith, linking ordinary and common things with the miraculous and remote; they can be like flames passing through filthy places, scorching, cleansing, growing in light by feeding on darkness.

When a man has ceased to find in the natural world material aims only; when, watching a flower, he can almost see the Artist's hand lift from the pencilling of its transparent veins; then he will have attained such strong freedom that he will stand already on the foothills of eternity, gazing with love and wonder into the complex life of nature, which is the life of God.

Once, on a clear winter day, a wide stretch of ploughland lay before me; it was beautiful in the rich colouring and fertility of its shallow, faintly shadowed furrows; but it was still and silent as nature seems to those who see nothing within and beyond it. Suddenly I was aware of swift, continual motion all over the brown land; up and down the furrows gleamed the white breasts of plovers. In a moment they rose with a flashing of underwings in the light, and their plaintive cry came down through the thin air. United to the soil by all the ties of life, being its very essence, they were yet much more; they were the soul of the field – gifted with music and motion and the freedom of the sky. So, at first, the patient watcher of earth sees only inanimate beauty, voiceless, without initiative. Then suddenly there is a clapping of wings, a flash of immortal radiance, a strange, haunting cry – and he has had a vision of the Soul of the World.

Populus Trémula

THE aspen stood with her feet in the deep-hidden well which she kept cool all summer. Close beside her, sheltering her from the coldest winds, was a wall of dark rock, where grew minute ferns and mountain speedwell and the bright wild strawberry and fragrant ground-ivy and rose-root. Above hung the thymy hill where dry grasses and bracken murmured or screamed in the wind, unsheltered far up there against the cold sky of early spring. In front, opposite the rock, was an old, tall, ragged hedge of elder and spindle, wild apple, honeysuckle, cornel and briar roses. Beyond was a pasture where the sheep lay, a farm, shrugged beneath the frost, a welter of wood and meadow stretching mile upon mile to the grave, dark, omnipresent hills. On the west an oakwood shelved. On the east was a buttress of the hill.

So the aspen, regnant over her little enclosure of quiet turf and leaf-mould, enjoyed a deep peace far below the bruit of the storm, a peace like that of the creatures in the secret well. The green sunrise, the voices of the plovers wailing for summer, cries from the farm, the sea-sound in the wood, the infinite faint murmur of the plain, were all known to the aspen. For the rich earth which had made the wheat, the doves and the song of the doves, the ethereal wild rose, the kestrel gazing sunward with unconquerable pride, had also made the aspen. She was their kin, and when she trembled, it was the plain that trembled. When she was torn, the plain bled. When her roots drank daintily of the well, she shared a sacrament of which earth and sky had compounded the wafer and the wine.

All winter the aspen had bent to the storm, black with rain, white with snow, dumbly enduring dark skies. But now the first lamb stood uncertainly on long legs in the home meadow, and mercury sprang startlingly green in the woods, and through the aspen's upper boughs, where the knobs of the buds swelled, ran a deep flush of gold. Oval, pale, between the hollows of mossed roots, in the soft, thick, wrinkled leaves, opened the first primrose on its rose-pink stalk. The hedge of cornel and briar-rose and elder and spindle quickened in tongues of pale fire. The aspen's little kingdom was strown with nosegays of starry celandine and dog violets and scattered, lengthening, pink-stalked primroses.

The sap ran strongly under the urgent compulsion of life. The flower-buds swelled. Suddenly the aspen burst into blossom, so that every yellow twig was hung with swaying rosy tassels, and the resinous sweetness of the broken buds made a deep atmosphere about the tree. Doves, brown as the buds, eyed the aspen with eyes as rosy as the flower tassels, and, alighting there, began to croon softly. Wood-pigeons from the western oak wood tossed down their brave notes like golden balls. Softly against the damp brown rock arose hyacinths, and pink-stained anemonies where the celandine had bloomed. But still, though ten thousand tassels swung like bridal garlands, the aspen had no song.

The young bracken stole upward. Pigeons were nesting. Plovers had forgotten their winter cry. The cuckoo had come. Through the white, soft wood of the tree life shuddered up, urgent as death itself, creative, insistent. Suddenly, amazingly, the aspen was in leaf. Small, soft and round, the folded leaves stood up from the twigs. Then, with demur that changed to assent, they drooped. And as they drooped they began to tremble, as if a heat-haze lingered over the tree. The aspen sighed. It was a sigh, faint as morning mist, but it was expression.

She waited. What would come? Every bird in the wood had found its solace. Every flower beneath the hill had known the sun. Fragrance and music went together across the plain like lovers unveiled. Earth and sky were cymbals, striking out life.

No one had rebuked the aspen. Still she waited, trembled, sighed. The woman dipping from the well sighed also as she heard the voice of her lover calling the herd from cropping cool grass beneath the hedge. She trembled beneath the shaken tree and spilt the bright blue water among the large, spent anemonies. The aspen recollected herself, ingathered. In all that musical sweet morning none had chidden her, nor at noon, nor when the shadows lengthened. When the crystal ball of the moon stood upon the hill and a clear light without colour tranced the plain, the cowman stole through the silence to keep his tryst. His cattle, wild with summer's glory, broke pasture and gambolled, soundless, on the moss with soundless shadows. And the aspen, aware of all, wrapt in all, knew that none would rebuke her, and lifting up her voice, silver with the green and white beauty of ten thousand leaves, tender and plashing and cool as crisp water over a fall, in the absolute, holy stillness, in the hush of heaven, she sang.

Fruits of the Earth

Fruits of the Earth

ON a bright, rook-haunted September morning, in the wide upland pastures where kestrels scream and the sheep cry across the dew, it is good to be astir very early. Then the rabbits and the young foxes are playing in the shadow at the wood's edge, magpies in the tall trees are calling to one another in their harsh voices, and the woodpecker's laughing note re-echoes. Every grass-blade and hedge, and the long, purple-jewelled blackberry vines are hung with white cobwebs sewn with diamonds, like elfin awnings. Even in October, when the last bee is gone and the fruits are sodden and frosted, the blackberry is lovely with leaves that burn from yellow to crimson. Not many scents are so rich, so racy of the soil, as the scent of blackberries and wimberries.

Of all wild fruits the wimberry, or cloud-berry, should rank first. Its colour is the bloomy purple of distant hills. It tastes of Faery. It will grow only in beautiful and mysterious places. High on the airy hill, far from any sound of village or hamlet, voice or bell – except the voice of the shepherd and the sheep-bell's silver tinkle – is the chosen haunt of the wimberry. Countless acres are covered with the neat, shining bushes, tall beside the streams, lowly on the summits. In spring, the leaf green is splashed with a beautiful red, like the colour of a ladybird; then come pink flowers, honeyed and waxen, and above their sweet acres the large, almost black bumble-bees of the hills coast to and fro with their deep murmur, like far-off

seas in a dream. At the end of June, when young curlews run among the bushes, like yellow chickens pen-
cilled with brown, the fruit begins to ripen, but it is
not often ready for picking until after Saint Swithin's.
From that date until late September a tide of life, gipsy
and cottager and dweller in the plain, flows up into our
hills. To the Stiperstones, to the Longmynd, to the
wild, lonely stretches of Clun Forest, come the stooping, neutral-tinted figures – the lads with their little
home-made trucks, the wise babies whose wimberry-
picking is not yet, and whose task is simply to be good.
Alone beside the family kettle amid the day's provisions
he sits, the baby, smiling, gazing trustfully at the blue,
arching sky, so deeply saturated with wimberry juice
that one doubts if many Saturday tubs will clean
him. He achieves the end and aim of his day: he
is good. On every side of him stretch the purple
plateaux, dotted with busy figures. Here and there,
at a lost signpost or a mountain ash, is the trysting-place of the wimberry higgler. Twice a week
he appears with his cart and his rough pony, and
over the green, deeply rutted tracks, down valleys
brimful of shadow and along precipitous roads,
the wimberries go on their journey to the cities of
England.

Cranberries grow on some of our hills, but sparsely,
in crevices of the black rock and on bare summits. The
polished leaves, the waxen-white blossoms, the large
coral-tinted berries, glow on their sombre background
like richly coloured statues of saints and Madonnas set
up in sorrowful places. Under grieved autumn skies,

amid bitter juniper and withered heather and riven rock, they achieve the beauty which is at once delicate and hardy, and they bless the gaunt solitudes where only the anxious sheep lift amber eyes as the cranberry picker passes, and only the hovering kestrel and the peregrine falcon, dark upon the driving sky, look down.

In the plain, when winter strips the hedges and the honeysuckle has not yet sent out her bright pairs of leaves, the fruited blackthorn reigns. She is a creature of dark weather. From her first adventure into a cold March world, with her gift of sweet, golden-anthered blossom, to her wintry ripening, she has no kinship with the luxurious daughters of summer. Not for her the slow-falling, scarlet fruit of August: but when the cherry and the apple have laid aside their beauty, she sets her black twigs with bloomy, purple fruit, austerely gorgeous. The berries give the impression of melting the frost by their rich warmth, and there is no fruit-gathering that brings more zest than the gathering of the sloe in the whistling hedges with a robin for company.

The fruit of the spindle-tree has a strangeness and an ancientry in its down-hanging, petalled cup of deep rose and orange. A tall, slender spindle set with shining pink lamps makes an exquisite, almost an exotic picture on a white-frost morning. No one plants the spindle now, but it must have been one of the October beauties of the countryside when in every home the busy hum of the spinning-wheels filled the fire-lit evening. It is to be found to-day in old woods and in hedges that have, with the lapse of time, ceased to be hedges and become grooves of trees. Soon, perhaps, it will be gone, like the sweet faces, the little hands, that once watched and tended the whispering wheels.

Once a year the elder attains perfect beauty. She paints her leaves with pale rose, primrose and gold, crimson and violet, and sets forth her fruits like elfin grapes. Then every elder is full of little wings, and shrill with small, thankful bird-notes. If there come a rainy day, the elder hangs beneath every purple berry a silver berry. Then woods grow vague in the thickened atmosphere, the courses of the streams are marked in mist, and on the first morning of sharp frost the painted curtains of the elder fall upon the grass.

It was in clear October weather, in a green valley beneath a steep, dark mountain, that I found the long avenue of fruited rowans growing on either side of a half-obliterated road where once marched the Romans. The trunks were gnarled and riven, but the trees stood against the hill, beneath the egg-shell sky, in the vital colours of youth. And all about them, like angels in a picture, hovered creatures winged with bright black and pale silver, creatures too eerily fair to be only blackbirds and thrushes. They seemed like spirits bound to the trees by a charm; and indeed the whole valley was bewitched, far gone in spells.

And so we come to the yew – the yew, that sets beneath her brooding branches a fruit vivid and unearthly, startling the eye inured to darkness with sudden living red, as if she lit, for comfort in the night, above the cold sleepers in her keeping, a galaxy of burning hearts.

Roots

Roots

NOW is the time when gardeners begin to 'delve and dyke, toil and sweat, turn the earth upside down and seek the deepnesse.' Now they begin to know their plants, not as summer acquaintances, but as friends. For the root is the plant. Into it is gathered the whole personality of the creature that slips up into the illuminated air every spring, and withdraws at the fall of the leaf, folding her beauty once more into that humble shelter where she subtly contrives her own creation. There lie, in tiniest miniature, in vaguest embryo, in secret recesses of nerve and fibre, the brittle or sappy stalks; the eager tendrils; the leaves of velvet or of silk, like fans or swords, hearted, pennoned, tented; petals ethereal or empurpled; nectary and filament and anther; golden bees' meat; mysterious ripening calyx and painted fruit. Therein is locked the very heart of spring, the scent that can enchant a summer night, the bread and wine of life's sacrament. A small seed rooted beneath the winter keeps in its silence the stir and murmur, the rustling music, the golden welter of harvest, with its heavy waggons, its shouts from the sacked field to the fragrant rickyard.

If there was one thing more than others in which the old herbalists had faith it was in the medicinal properties of roots. With the relentless thoroughness of the medieval mind they preferred things in essence, and they liked their drugs to be as strong as possible. Though so many roots are still used medicinally, some have fallen into disrepute, and all are used more mercifully. The modern chemist would not entirely approve of either method in the following recipe for using the roots of the crimson peony. This was a sovereign cure for several diseases. You simply cut the root into thin slices and hung it round the patient's neck. 'If this fails,' adds the herbalist, with a scepticism that must have been deprecated by the religious people of his day, 'if this fails, reduce it to powder and make the patient swallow a dram thrice daily, until he is cured of his fits.' How well one can hear him say this – between clenched teeth, as it were, with the furious materialism of those who fall from the heights of spiritualism! How well one can see the relentless scene of dosing that occurred thrice daily – worthy of Hogarth's painting – and how one can sympathize with the patient, who must have so greatly preferred faith-healing! Lily-roots were boiled in milk and were emollient; wild lettuce was for dropsy; colchicum and the milky juice of the wild white convolvulus were for nervous disorders. Nerves were very much discouraged in old days, and the roots of half the plants in England seem to have been called to their aid. With a belief in the efficacy of pain to heal and cure, the herbalists chose for their medicaments such roots as that of the purple pasque flower, which cured blindness, but gave 'a severe, lancinating pain.' And surely they were wise. The roots of life are nourished on pain, and whoever participates in this love-feast of reality must suffer. The butterfly knows nothing of the conflict, the grief of the root struggling with earth in darkness, yet only through the bravery of the root, its determination to suffer rather than die, does the flower dance in the light. It is the love of the root, dumbly struggling, that creates splendours the root will never see, splendours which it dreams, all alone in the dark.

In a dim alley somewhere near Paternoster Row is a small window artlessly piled with bulbs and roots of those strange tints and textures in which these beings of the underworld love to wrap themselves. The owner of the shop has forsworn flowers. Instead, he sets forth mottled beans like jewels, ruby-tinted; many-coloured bulbs; the reserved but all-promising dahlia. And he is wise. A flower we see; we can touch its silk and smell its fragrance. But a root! A root is the unknown; it holds the future; it shares the allure of the horizon, where anything wonderful may haunt; it gives nothing, but it hints of untold gifts. The bulbs glow with a dim, rich lustre. There are brown tulip bulbs, dapper and well-found; straw-coloured narcissi; pale globular daffodils; autumn crocuses that will send up, naked and brave, their flowers to fill the September meadows with magic; tiger-lilies, wherein is caged savage colour; hyacinths, prophesying of their future tints by the red and rose and primrose of their crinkled tissue wrappings which are like the luminous paper of Christmas cards, that sheds on angels or Holy Families mysterious coloured lights; white lilies, their pale and flaking bulbs heavy with the June glories of great chalices and golden pollen, recalling in their stately promise a herd of white milch kine. There are the anemones, with tubers utterly reserved, unlovely, shrivelled; yet, like those unfortunate ladies of the old dangerous years, who were turned into hags by perverse wizards, they keep surprises of beauty hidden for him that has faith and gives them leave to bloom.

No wonder that dusty window in the roar of the City traffic takes away one's breath with its 'whence?' and 'whither?' its secrecy, its conserved sweetness! Looking at these silent beings that have come out of the earth, that will return to the earth, that hold their gifts of beauty within invisible treasuries, keeping somewhere between minute sap-runnels and sad-coloured layers of fibrous substance the riddle of the universe in little, we are confronted with a miracle as heart-stirring, as tear-compelling as any in the sweet Galilean story. Dead and cold as a pebble seems the crocus bulb, yet come the white points, the bursting green of young leaves, the folded golden flag, the chalice, superbly frail, drawing to itself the music of bees, cool dews, sunlight. Looking at its triumph, the imagination is fired; we hear a voice, stern with the wonder of its own power, speaking across centuries of time and masses of dead matter, from furthest space or from our own hearts, calling low, but with a most compelling sweetness – '*Talitha cumi!*'

There is a more vital joy in dealing with the roots of plants than can ever be found in communion with the flower alone. What summer nosegay has the good smell of primrose roots or violet roots torn asunder for replanting of bruised lilies, of ploughman's spikenard? It is not only the roots of the cedar that 'give a good smell'; dig up any root and you will have an earthy fragrance which is neither that of earth nor rain nor of the flower nor the leaf, but wholly individual. The marvellous sweetness in the air of an autumn day is not chiefly of late summer flowers, nor of wet earth, nor of fruits and fading leaves, nor of corn – though ripe corn does often steep the whole countryside in golden fragrance. It is the roots, delved for and bruised and subjected to the shock of air and sunlight, and pouring out their strange, heady fragrances on these autumn days only. It is a lesson in reality to see, when you have known all summer the ethereal beauty of white clematis or honeysuckle, the roots clutching with a hundred tiny hands the dark soil. Not the whitest rose, not the frailest lily can ignore the earth. There are curious plants that have a whimsey to deny earth, to touch it only at second-hand – the mistletoe, that prefers to touch earth only when it is transformed into apple wood or apricot wood; the broomrape, that goes to the broom and clover and ivy and says, 'Nourish me; I am too dainty for the crude earth.' But what are they? The mistletoe is a poor, colourless thing; the broomrape has not a leaf on it, and is as near ugliness as a plant can be. Even that most unearthly of flowers, the white water-lily, floating on deep water, is anchored far below in the black river bed. Every one of those wide spreading leaves, those pure blossoms, has its long, swaying root going down into darkness.

Whether those algae that cause the 'Breaking of the Meres' every year in Shropshire should be called plants or not the writer does not know; but these do seem to root in the water itself, rising suddenly to the surface, flinging out filaments like roots, and thus causing a boiling in the lake which has been compared to the scriptural 'troubling of the waters.' But such things are the exception. The rule is that the more delicate and beautiful the flower and fruit the closer must be the union with earth. And the point of contact is the root. There colour and scent are made; there the hundred-foot tree lies in little; there the petal that a dewdrop almost destroys is held safe under the ponderous earth. In the root, when April comes, Someone awakes, rubs drowsy eyes, stretches drowsy hands, remembers a dream of light that troubled its sleep, and begins, with infinite precautions, finesse and courage, to work the miracle of which it has knowledge; 'eagerly watching for its flower and fruit, anxious its little soul looks out.'

Surely no idea of God could so well hint of Him as this idea of the root – of the great root of a forest tree, hawsered in the heart of matter; upholding matter; transforming matter by a secret alchemy into beauty that goes out from mystery – lives its day – returns, weary, into mystery, and is again renewed.

'None can tell how from so small a centre come such sweets.'

The Crockman

The Crockman

THE Crockman journeys along quiet lanes and hill-tracks, and as a rule the small market town in the centre of a lonely district is the largest place he ever sees. As his name implies, he sells china – or, rather, rough earthenware, deep red, partly glazed milk-bowls, yellow butter-crocks, blue and white barrel milk-jugs and 'semi-porcelain' cups and saucers such as are used in farmhouses and cottages.

He sells salt too, which is always in demand. A bar of salt, in addition to the huge basket of groceries, is too much even for the strong arms of 'mother,' as she starts courageously home on market day, coming first by carrier's cart, which sets her down a mile or so from home. So she is glad to have the salt brought to her door.

A strong float, like a coster's cart, is the Crockman's vehicle. It is drawn by an old pony bought for a song, or by a hill pony broken-in at home. The float looks gay careering along bleak hillsides, down misty valleys, and drawing up with a flourish before the open door of the farm. There is a subdued clashing of ware. If it is sunny, the daffodil-tinted bowls and terra-cotta buttermits glow like jewels. The salt sparkles. Willow-pattern dishes shine cleanly. Out comes the Missus. She buys a bar of salt, six pitcher eggs, and a large pot-bellied beer-jug with red flowers painted on it, because the maister's jug was broken last harvest. The bargaining over, the Crockman has a mug of ale, or, if there is prosperation on the farm, a sit-down knife-and-fork tea with bacon and potatoes.

On market day in his metropolis the Crockman renews his stores, spreads his wares on straw in the market, generally in the open air, and from the rostrum of an orange box proceeds to sell them.

When his great voice goes roaring down the busy aisles a crowd gathers – lads with straws in their mouths, old ladies in white aprons and vast brooches of polished stone, girls with butter baskets, shepherds whose calm will probably be undisturbed by Judgment Day, children with gingerbread in their mouths and on their persons.

The Crockman holds up a large willow-pattern dish.

'Tuppence.'

'Fi'pence.'

'Ladies and gents, this is 'eartbreaking! The biggest dish ever I sold! You can put half a sheep on it if you've a mind. Ladies, *if* you please!'

'A tanner.'

'Ten three fardens.'

'Now, now, people all, you're laughing at poor Jack. Ten-three for a dish worth five shilling?'

'A bob.'

The bidding stops.

'The Ten Commandments,' says the Crockman, 'you may forget and welcome. But meanness I cannot abide. A bob for my beautiful dish? People, I'd sooner *break* it!'

And holding it high above his head he sends it crashing on to the pavement.

Who is to know, unless the Crockman tells the secret, that the dish was 'flawed seconds' and only intended for this dramatic moment?